LOKPAL BILL

LOKPAL BILL

ANNA'S MOVEMENT THAT SHOOK INDIA

Sashi B. Sahai

KALPAZ

Lokpal Bill

ISBN: 978-81-7835-947-2

Published in 2014 in India by
Kalpaz Publications
C - 30 Satyawati Nagar
Delhi - 110052
E-mail: kalpaz@hotmail.com
Phone : 9212142040

Leser Type setting : Lucky Graphic, Delhi
Printed at : Sagar Color Scan, Delhi

Contents

	Preface	7
	Acknowledgements	9
	Introducation	11
1.	The Anna Hazare Phenomenon	15
2.	The Ramdeo Interlude	21
3.	The Lokpal Campaign Back with a Bang	27
4.	A Million Mutinies	31
5.	The Truce and The Impact	38
6.	Background of Anti-corruption Legislation in India	45
7.	History of Lokpal Bills that were Aborted	49
8.	Beginning of Ministers' Misconduct	55
9.	Scam After Scam	60
10.	Critical Issues of The Lokpal Debate	76
11.	Loopholes in the Anti-corruption Regime	92
12.	The Institutional Loophole	97
13.	CBI: The Kingpin of Anti-corruption Mechanism	104
14.	Ombudsman in Different Countries	111
15.	Electoral Reforms	116
16.	The Cause Betrayed	121
17.	2G Spectrum Scam	127
18.	Extent and Magnitude of Corruption in India	134
19.	Lokpal as an Agent of Good Governance	152

20. The Unending Lokpal Debate 179

21. 'Coalgate' or Coal Block Allocations Scam 183

22. Anna's Movement at the Cross Road 190

23. Kejriwal's New Avatar as a Political Leader 194

24. The Show Goes on 202

25. Augusta Westland Chopper Scam 216

26. Corruption in India : A Question 233

27. Judicial Activism Against Corruption and Criminalisation 238

Preface

In writing this book on Lokpal as the anti corruption watchdog, I have come a full circle in my stint as a writer. For, my first book published in 1995, entitled "Politics of Corruption" was also about the same issue. It would appear to be a coincidence that I am ending up at where I began my writing adventure, now that I am in the sunset years of my life.

But it is not a mere co-incidence. For I have been so much obsessed with the issue of corruption in public life that I hardly miss an opportunity to give vent to my anguish against it. Not because I have been a victim of corruption personally, but because I have encountered it in a big way in my professional life.

So when my publisher, Kalpaz Publications, suggested that I write on the issue of Lokpal, at the height of Anna's anti- corruption movement, I could not resist the urge to do it. I had one doubt, however, which I shared with him. The Lokpal stir was like a bubble, I thought, which would burst in a short time ending readers interest in it. But my publisher, a seasoned professional in his own line, was confident that the issue would remain live for quite some time sustaining readers interest in it. And, as it turned out at the end of 2013, he was right. That is why Kalpaz Publications has established itself among the top publishing houses of Delhi.

And yet, with all my compelling desire to record my views on the issue, it turned out to be a tough job. Once the Lokpal debate erupted with Anna Hazare's three days fast at Janter Manter, Delhi in April 2011, events started moving so fast that it was difficult to keep pace with them. Covering the fast moving developments through pen and paper was almost like making a running commentary on a cricket match.

That too was possible only with the help of the internet. Thanks to the keenness of all the stake-holders in the marathon Lokpal debate, the government, Anna's team and others, to place their records on the Net, these could be easily accessed in course of the writing. That made it possible to keep abreast of the arguments and counter arguments put forward by parties engaged in the Lokpal debate.

Finally, I would like to record my gratitude to my friends and relatives who accessed the Net for me to pile me with enough matter to keep on writing. Because being an old fashioned pen pusher, surfing the Net was beyond my capacity.

Sashi B. Sahai

Acknowledgements

Apart from an internet savvy family member who provided me with relevant inputs by surfing the net, I would like to record my gratitude to Sri D.P. Ojha IPS (Retd.), former D.G.P. and Vigilance Chief of Bihar. A long time professional colleague of mine, he rendered valuable assistance in writing this book through frequent interaction in course of writing. A known crusader against corruption, he fought many a legal battles in High Court and Supreme Court to assert the right of Vigilance agencies to investigate corruption cases without any check by higher bureaucracy and their political bosses. He made some valuable suggestions which have been incorporated in the book, besides helping in getting some chapters typed and corrected.

Sashi B. Sahai

Introduction

There is nothing new about corruption on the part of public servants in our country. It is an old and chronic malady which was taken note of by our ancients. Kautilya, the author of 'Arthashtra', a Mauryan Manual of governance, observes: "Just as it is impossible not to taste honey or poison that finds itself at the tip of the tongue, so it is impossible for a government servant not to eat up at least a bit of the king's revenue. Just as with fish moving under water it cannot possibly be discerned whether they are drinking water or not, so it is impossible to detect government servants employed on official duties when helping themselves to money."

Kautilya's caustic observation underlines the fact that we the people of India have been co-existing with the evil of public servants' corruption since ancient times. This has been noted by foreign observers who have tried to delve into the mystique of Indian reality in modern times. Ronald Segal, an acclaimed foreign writer, has in his book, "The crisis of India" has gone to the extent of observing "corruption in India is sanctified by tradition." Earlier, Robert Clive, the predator colonial ruler of India during East India Company days, had proclaimed that corruption was a way of life in India. Clive had indulged in crudest form of corruption and bribery to enrich himself while posted as Governor General under the East India Company. Sardar K.M. Parnikar's description of the East India Company's regime in Bengal during 1765-1772 as a "robber state" referred not only to the company's administration in general but was particularly appropriate in regard to the rapacious conduct of Robert Clive. When he was-hauled up by British Parliament for his corrupt ways, he came out with the plea that corruption was a way of life in India.

Clive's assertion was based on his own experience of the ease with which he enriched himself by extracting illegal presents and bribes during his tenure in India without any resistance or check. That underlines the easy acceptability of bribery and corruption by the people of India which is the crux of the corruption syndrome of the country. In sharp contrast, Clive himself was roundly criticised by British Parliament for his corrupt practices in India. It was his successor Warren Hastings, who had continued with Clive's tradition of using his official position to make money for himself, who faced the brunt of British Parliament's condemnation of his indulgence in corruption. Edmund Burke led a crusade against him in British Parliament and in 1780, the House of Commons passed a resolution for his recall from India. That only highlights the intense sensitivity of British society to corruption indulged in by its own representative in India.

By way of course correction of British rule in India, they appointed Lard Cornwallis as the head of the government in India who was not only himself above corruption but initiated measures to suppress bribery and corruption. Towards this end, he stopped the evil of private trade by employees of East India Company and required each officer to declare his assets under oath before leaving India. He enforced these directives strictiy and dismissed some high officials in the process. With their ill-gotten wealth, many of the company's officials had bought up bogus parliamentary constituencies in England which came to be known as "pocket boroughs". The British Parliament tackled this problem by passing the Reform Act of 1832 by which these "rotten boroughs" were deprived of representation in the House of Commons.

Author major reform introduced by the British colonial regime in 1856 was selection of East India Company's officials sent to India on merit through competition. This resulted in drastic change for the better in the caliber and integrity of civil servants working in India. By the second half of the 19th century, the Indian Civil Service (ICS) flowered into an institution which came to be regarded as model of integrity and competence. Some of the outstanding men of the ICS were Charles Metcalfe, Elphinstone, Vincent Smith and of course A.O. Hume, the founder of Indian National Congress.

It is in respect of these illustrious men that Philip Mason in his book "The Men who Ruled India" quotes Plato in the introduction. He says that the civil servants sent out to govern India were brought up on Plato. Because "Plato pictured a state ruled by guardians, superior to the ties of marriage or fatherhood and to the attraction of gold..........." These officials set high standards of personal conduct and integrity, apart from efficiency and performance.

It must be understood that the British debunked the corrupt and installed those of high integrity not particularly for the benefit of their subjects in India, but because corruption as such was not acceptable to the British society. It was on account of their inacceptability of corruption on the part of public servants that they replaced the corrupt by honest civil servants who stood for probity in public life. Thus the empire-builders of a foreign land cleaned up their act in India and ended up handing over a remarkably clean and corruption free administration to the leaders of independent India.

But what happened after that? Within 60 years of independence we find ourself trapped in the cesspool of corruption. And this in spite of the fact that our first generation nation - builders started off with the highest standards of probity and purity in public life. How come? What went wrong? The answer lies in our overall permissiveness and readiness to co-exist with corruption. In other words, we seem to accept corruption on the part of public functionaries as an unavoidable evil. It is our acceptability of corruption as a part of life which has landed the nation in the mire of corruption. It is not that our people are corrupt as some foreign observers have commented. The vast majority of Indians are not the practitioners but victims of corruption. It is not that "Corruption in India is sanctified by tradition", as Ronald Segal has observed. It is our smugness and silence in the face of corruption which has been misunderstood as our approval of corruption.

This book is about the breaking the silence of the common man and piercing the smog of permissiveness surrounding the canker of corruption eating into the vitals of our body politic. It gives a blow by blow account of how a dedicated group of anti-corruption crusaders - Anna Hazare, Arvind Kejriwal and co - tore apart the curtain of acceptability covering the running sore of corruption in India for centuries. Never before in history was so much done to expose Corruption as an unmixed evil. The anti-corruption crusaders led by Anna Hazare have in fact heralded the dawn of a new era by proclaiming loud and clear that corruption was no longer acceptable to the people of India. At the least, they have succeeded in putting eradication of corruption at the top of the nation's agenda. This book dwells upon the hows and whys of this seminal change in the corruption syndrome of India in the second decade of the 21st century.

1

The Anna Hazare Phenomenon

Anna Hazare ? Who? That would have been the reaction of common man in India beyond his home state of Maharashtra before April 2011. No longer so after that. Once this less known social activist based in his decrepit home village Ralegan Siddhi, about 100 km from Pune, launched his campaign for an effective Lokpal Bill to curb corruption, Anna Hazare became a household name in the country.

For Anna Hazare, fight against corruption and other social evils was nothing new. In fact, he had been a fighter all through his life at multiple fronts. After enlisting in the Indian Army in the wake of the India-China War of 1962, he had faced the enemy bullets on the battle front during Indo-Pak war of 1965 and narrowly survived. After opting for voluntary retirement from the Indian Army in 1978, he made his humble home village Ralegan Siddhi his base to fight against all kinds of social evils. In the process, he succeeded in eradicating the menace of drinking among the village youth by pushing out the liquor vendors who had a vice like grip over them. He was also instrumental in introducing rain water conservation in his drought prone village to the great relief of his co-villagers.

With all his reforming zeal, his prime target was governmental corruption, which was eating into the vitals of economic development and distorting the morals of the people. To fight corruption, he founded an organisation known as people's movement against Corruption. In furtherance of this movement, he gave up his Padmashri Award in April 1994 to protest a corruption scandal involving Rs. 50 lakhs in social forestry department of Maharashtra government. His protest was against the inaction of the state government in the matter even though he had provided what he considered adequate evidence on the scam to the Chief Minister in 1990 itself. In 1995-96, he had forced the government of Maharashtra to drop two Cabinet Ministers on charges of corruption.

Anna Hazare had thus been an untiring campaigner against corruption at the state level in his own way. This time round, as the graph of corruption scandals in the country was touching new heights, he extended the scope of his campaign to the national level early in April 2011. The move was well taken by the public as the country at this time was sizzling under the heat of serial corruption scandals-Adarsh Housing Society scam, Commonwealth Games scam, 2G Spectrum allotment scam, etc. He revived the proposal of setting up the institution of Lokpal (Ombudsman) often talked about but left cooling in the cold storage of Parliament for over 40 years. It may be noted that the U.P.A government had prepared the draft of a Lokpal Bill in 2010, but failed to introduce it in Parliament. It was in this background that Anna Hazare assembled a team of eminent members of civil society to draft a fresh Bill with provisions for comprehensive powers to Lokpal proposed to be installed to curb corruption. The Bill was drafted by N. Santosh Hegde, a retired Judge of Supreme court and erstwhile Lokayukta of Karnataka, Prashant Bhushan, a senior Supreme Court lawyer and well-known public interest litigation activist, along with India Against corruption movement members. It was termed as the Jan Lokpal Bill (People's Ombudsmen Bill).

Having come up with the concrete draft of the proposed Bill, Anna was reasonable enough to offer a dialogue with the government on the subject. The government faltered and failed to respond positively. At this stage, Anna's simple demand was to form a joint committee of representatives of the government of India and civil society to draw up an effective Lokpal Bill to be introduced in Parliament. There was nothing extra-constitutional about the demand. But the ruling party politicians started questioning the locus standi of Anna's team in formulating the Bill which they claimed was the exclusive prerogative of Parliament. The argument was evidently flawed because Anna never challenged the supremacy of Parliament. He only wanted an effective Lokpal Bill to be drafted by a joint committee of the ministers and concerned members of the civil society and put up in Parliament. Anna clearly affirmed that he would accept the verdict of Parliament. Where was the question of undermining the supremacy of Parliament in this simple suggestion which the ruling politicians sought to make out?

It was at this point that the U.P.A. government willy-nilly put itself virtually in an adversary relationship with Anna's anti-corruption movement. The ruling political leaders did not want to be seen as such though. For they were conscious of the growing public outrage at corruption scandals against which Anna's campaign was directed. This resulted in kind of a schizophrenia in their approach to Anna's movement and interaction with his team. It continued to dog them all through their handling of the situation.

The initial reaction of the government was to outright reject the demand for a joint drafting committee headed by a civil society activist. That acted as a catalyst for the turbulent events to follow which shook the political establishment. Anna promptly responded by sitting on a fast unto death at Jantar Mantar in Delhi beginning 5 April 2011. He declared "I will fast until Jan Lokpal Bill is passed". That signaled the onset of an anti-corruption storm which swept across the whole country as never before.

The impact was immediate and instant. The numerous electronic news channels throughout the country lapped it up as a golden opportunity to improve their T.R.P. ratings. The print media did not lag behind. As a result, thousands of people across the country came up in loud support of Anna's effort. More than a hundred sat on a fast at different venues. Leading opinion-makers in India from all walks of life-film makers, actors, music directors, spiritual leaders, cricketers, etc., voiced their vocal support for Anna Hazare through social networking websites or the media. Prominent among them were Amitabh Bachchan, Aamir Khan, Shabana Azmi, A.R. Rahman, Sri Ravi Shankar, Swami Agnivesh and cricketer Kapil Dev. Film maker Pritish Nandy and actors Anupam Kher and Tom Alter actually visited Jantar Mantar where

Anna was sitting on fast. Summing up the position, the '*The Economic Times*' (9 April 2011) observed. "A total of 4.4. million tweets from 8,26,000 unique users across 79 cities in India in just three days. That is just a sample of Indian sentiments on line for Anna Hazare and his crusade against corruption".

The tremendous support that Anna attracted through his fast was not lost upon the government. Running *with the hare and hunting with the* hound, which characterised the government's approach to Anna's movement all through, Govt. hesitatingly acceded to the main demand for a joint drafting committee with a rider that the committee would be headed by a Minister of the government. Anna had no problem with this rider. He agreed that five members each from the government and his civil society activists constitute the Joint Drafting Committee with a senior Minister as Chairman and a citizen activist as Co-chairman.

While the agreement brought a great relief to the harried political leadership, it was celebration time for Anna and his supporters. His fast at Jantar Mantar which began on 5 April 2011 ended at 10.30 A.M on 9 April 2011 on a dramatic note. Anna first offered sips of water to some women supporters who had fasted along with him. He then took a glass of juice from the hand of a five year old girl Soumya Kohli who had been brought to the place by her father on this hallowed occasion. And thousands of his supporters who had gathered at Jantar Mantar went into raptures singing and dancing to celebrate what they perceived to be people's victory over arrogant wielders of political power. In the evening, large numbers turned up at India Gate with candle lights and national flags in their hands singing patriotic songs and calling upon people to join the fight against corruption.

Many ruling politicians and some commentators with blinkered vision sought to dismiss the spontaneous popular support for Anna as contrived "tamasha", some dubbed it as a creation of the hyper active media. Needless to say, this was nothing more than an utterly futile exercise in self-deception. If they thought that by indulging in such wild prouncements they were going to discredit Anna, they were awfully wide off the mark. Instead of belittling Anna, every such pronouncement discredited them instead and added to the charisma of Anna and legitimacy of his movement. Evidently, they were totally ignorant of the deep anger of the common man at the prevailing milieu of corruption in the country against which Anna was viewed as a lone warrior. The more they sought to discredit Anna, the more he rose in the esteem of the people as a knight in shining armour out to take on the demon of corruption head long. More of it later.

In fact, Anna himself must have been pleasantly surprised at nation wide euphoria at the initial success of his movement which catapulted him to the status of a national hero. It was not on account of his personality as such, as in the case of other national luminaries-past and present. (There was nothing elitist or glamorous about him. Far from it. In terms of formal education, he had not done even his high school when he joined the Army as a soldier truck-driver to earn a living). Nor was it on account of the modality of his anti-corruption campaign that is, sitting on a hunger strike (Every now and then, all kinds of people in India resort to fasting to vent their grievances and press for one demand or the other). Anna was hailed all over the country on account of the cause for which he launched his movement and resorted to fasting-eradication of corruption. It was an index of people's intense resentment against mounting surge of corruption and official inaction.

Sensing the mood of the people, the Prime Minister made a pious statement hailing the coming together of the government and civil society (Anna's team) to formulate a Lokpal Bill for introduction in Parliament. The joint drafting committee for Lokpal Bill, demanded by Anna and conceded by the government, came into being in April 2011. It comprised five Central Ministers from the government side and five civil society activists led by Anna Hazare. The government contingent was headed by Pranab Mukherjee and included P. Chidambaram, Veerappa Moily, Salman Khurshid and Kapil Sibal. The civil society team consisted of Anna Hazare himself and Shanti Bhushan, his lawyer son Prashant Bhushan, Santhosh Hegde and Arvind Kejriwal.

While the government representatives in the committee were well known Cabinet Ministers, the civil society members need a brief introduction about their status and background. Anna Hazare, the doyen of them all, needs no introduction. Shanti Bhushan, the senior most among them, was a veteran lawyer politician who was the law Minister in Morarji Desai's Janata Party Cabinet of 1977. His son Prashant Bhushan was an eminent Supreme Court lawyer in his own right well known as a public interest litigation activist. Santosh Hegde was a retired Judge of the Supreme Court and erstwhile Lok Ayukta of Karnataka. The youngest and least known among them was Arvind Kejriwal. An IIT Kharagpur alumni, Kejriwal joined the Indian Revenue Service after successfully competing in the U.P.S.C examination. But he had other idea of his mission in life. He went on study leave for two years after which he resigned from service to devote full time to social service. He distinguished himself as a Right to Information activist and was bestowed with the prestigious Magsaysay Award.

2

The Ramdev Interlude

Hardly had the heat and dust of Anna's four day fast over Lokpal Bill subsided, another anti-corruption heat wave started from another direction. Even as the Joint Drafting Committee was dragging its feet on hammering out a worthwhile Lokpal Bill draft by indulging in fruitless debates, another crusader against corruption emerged on the scene with a different agenda. It was yoga guru Ramdeo who took up the issue of black money stashed away by corrupt Indians including politicians in foreign, specially Swiss Banks. Subramaniam Swamy, President of the defunct Janata Party and lone whistle blower of corruption scandals, had earlier highlighted the issue of black money of Indian politicians in Swiss Banks. He had moved the Supreme Court to ask the government to disclose the names of Indian citizens having secret accounts in Swiss Banks. This had queered the pitch for Baba Ramdeo to launch his campaign against foreign bank deposits of corrupt Indians in a big way.

Yoga Guru Ramdeo grabbed the opportunity with both hands to launch his own crusade against corruption on this issue. Anna Hazare had already aroused the people to a high pitch over the sensitive issue of corruption. Ramdeo jumped into the fray with his own brand of anti corruption movement focusing on foreign bank accounts of the corrupt. The people were seething with anger against the merchants of black money believed to have drained the country of its wealth. Wild claims were made by the protesters against foreign bank deposits of the rich and about the volume of such deposits. It was proclaimed to be so big that, if brought back to the country it could vastly improve the economic condition of the people. Right or wrong, such tall claims had instant appeal among the gullible people of India who rose in support of Ramdeo's movement.

There was another favourable factor which attracted people to Ramdeo and his campaign. As an accomplished practitioner of yoga shining in the reflected glory of the legendry ancient yogi, Patanjali and beamed on the electronic media across, the country, Swami Ramdeo already had a big following of his own. To start with, therefore, he was ahead of Anna who was not really known outside Maharashtra before he batted for the long neglected instrument of Lokpal to curb corruption. There was thus an inbuilt ground swell of support for Ramdeo's campaign against black money stacked in foreign banks. Hordes of his unseen followers who had benefited from his yogic exercises beamed over TV Channels readily joined his bandwagon once he launched his movement.

Ramdeo had already been raising his voice against the scourge of corruption corroding the political system when Anna Hazare broke forth on the scene with his Lokpal agenda. Just as Anna's campaign came to a temporary stop following the constitution of Joint Drafting Committee for Lokpal Bill in April 2011, Ramdeo announced his resolve to fast into death over the issue of black money in Swiss Banks. Having burnt their fingers in Anna's four day fast over the issue of corruption, the ruling political leaders desperately wanted to stall another such fasting in the national capital. So when Ramdeo landed at Delhi early in June 2011 to launch his fast, four senior ministers of the government met him at the Airport. They sought to pursuade him to desist from resorting to his planned fast. Two Ministers met him again a day before the proposed fast on 4 June 2011 in an effort to convince him that the government was taking all steps to bring back black money kept in Swiss Banks.

What actually transpired in the ministers interaction with Ramdeo is not exactly known. Apparently, there was some kind of an initial agreement that Ramdeo would resort only to a token fast on the assurance that the government would take prompt action to retrieve black money in Swiss Banks. But the agreement did not work. Ramdeo accused that the government did not keep its word while the government spokesmen blamed Ramdeo for breach of the agreement. Any how, Ramdeo began his fast in a big yoga camp organised at Delhi's Ramlila ground which attracted a large crowd of his followers. Evidently, the government had landed itself in a mess. It was in a bind.

The political leadership had two options before it. It could allow Ramdeo's fast and the yoga camp to continue and persevere with the dialogue process initiated earlier. In the alternative, it could do what politicians in power always do to deal with a large public protest they do not want to continue-let the police break it up. The Government panicked and opted for the latter. It did not know that once the police *lathi* (stick) is let loose to disperse a public gathering by force, it does not know when and where to stop. Or perhaps, it knew and calculated that any blame for excessive use of force could conveniently be passed on to the local police functionaries.

What followed was not only unfortunate but also counter-productive in terms of the government's image in regard to the fight against corruption. And, a little dramatic too. As usually happens in this kind of an operation, lathi-wielding policemen fell upon the peaceful and half-sleepy gathering of Ramdeo's followers, including women and children, after midnight on 5 June 2011. They used their lathi without any check or inhibition to break up the ostensible yoga camp. Scores of people suffered severe lathi blows and many received grievous injuries. Rajbala, a housewife disciple of Ramdeo, sustained spinal injuries for which she had to be admitted to the intensive care unit of a government hospital in Delhi (She expired later after prolonged treatment). Ramdeo himself jumped from the podium in a women's dress to avoid the police lathi and escaped from the ground. He later explained that he apprehended threat to his life as the prime target of the police at the instance of the Home Ministry. Thus ended Ramdeo's infructuous campaign against foreign bank deposits of corrupt Indians. But not without leaving a trail of bitterness against the ruling dispensation.

The principal opposition party took up the issue of police

lathi charge on the peaceful gathering in a big way. Sushma Swaraj, the leader of the opposition in Lok Sabha, promptly visited the injured in hospital to express sympathy. She along with Arun Jaitley, her counterpart in Rajya Sabha, held a joint press conference denouncing the police lathi charge as a barbaric reminder of the infamous emergency days. The next day, BJP organised a 24 hours sit in at Raj Ghat, the sacred ground of Mahatma Gandhi's cremation, to register the party's strong protest against the government.

Anna Hazare also joined the chorus of protest against the use of what he termed as "brutal force" to disperse the peaceful gathering in Ramdeo's camp. To express his support for Ramdeo's anticorruption drive and sympathy for the victims of police lathi charge, Anna actually under took a one day fast in the wake of the unsavoury event. In a sudden twist, while the sound and fury of Anna's trumpet for his Jan Lokpal Bill dimmed for the time being (to be turned into a roar shortly), the loud thump of Ramdeo's tirade against Swiss Bank deposits rocked the national capital.

The print and electronic media lapped it up gratefully as a major bonanza. It turned out to be real boom time in the business of news reporting. TV channels vied with each other to display the midnight drama being enacted in Ramlila ground. The bizarre scene at the venue of Ramdeo's camp was beamed live by different TV channels, each trying to out do the other by making it more saucy. In the process, viewers across the country saw the entire episode of police beating up hapless men women and children gathered in the camp at midnight. All of them were not anti-corruption campaigners. Many, especially women and children like the fatally injured Rajbala, had come to the camp to see the revered yoga guru face to face. The viewers were aghast at the sight of Guru Ramdeo himself jumping from the podium in a women's dress to avoid being beaten up by lathi wielding policemen rampaging through the ground.

While the TRP rating of multiple TV channels soared sky

high, the popularity index of the government and its leading lights slumped to a new low. They had barely managed to come out of the imbroglios over Anna's Lokpal Bill earlier only to land themselves in another mess, largely of their own creation. The remarkable fact about Anna's and Ramdeo's campaigns was that both were directed against rampant corruption. And the ruling political leadership handled or mishandled them so clumsily as to create an impression that the government was against the anti-corruption movement as such. Right or wrong, it appeared to the people at large that the government was fighting against those who were out to fight against corruption. Nothing could be more damaging to the image of a ruling political dispensation in a democratic society widely conscious of prevailing corruption.

There was another ugly dimension to the government mishandling of Ramdeo's campaign - the ruthless lathi charge on an entirely peaceful congregation of Ramdeo's followers at midnight. No police or criminal code could justify this kind of action in a civilised society. No wonder that the principal opposition party cried foul likening it to police high handedness during the dreaded Emergency regime. TV viewers throughout the country were outraged at the sight of sitting or sleeping people, including women and children, being dragged and beaten up by lathi wielding police men at dead of night for no fault of theirs.

So much so that the country's highest judiciary, the Supreme Court of India, took suo motto notice of the matter on the basis of media reports. It directed the government/ Delhi police to explain what made them resort to lathi charge at a peaceful gathering including women and children at dead of night.

The unfortunate event also impacted the temporarily stalled Anna's campaign for adoption of his Lokpal Bill. As noted earlier, Anna had under taken a day's fast in protest against the breaking up of Ramdeo's camp with brutal force. It induced him to toughen his stand on the Lokpal Bill issue in the on-going negotiations with the government. As a result, another meeting of the Joint

Drafting Committee ended in a stalemate with both the government and Anna's representatives sticking to their respective positions. Anna, there upon, declared that if his Jan Lok Pal Bill was not introduced in the parliament session beginning first August 2011, he would sit on a fast unto death on 16 August. This laid the ground for a major confrontation between the government and Anna's group of civil society activists which swayed the country for well over a fortnight in August 2011 as never before. More about it in the next Chapter.

3

The Lokpal Campaign Back with a Bang

In the intergennum between the April agreement between Government and Anna and opening of Parliament session in August, the futile exercise of working out an agreed Lokpal Bill draft continued. Starting with the first meeting of the Joint Drafting committee on 16 April 2011, there were a series of meetings between the two sides without any result.

The minutes of the meetings of the Joint Drafting Committee make an interesting reading. There was much tall talk by the government representatives, that is the ministers, on the supremacy of the constitution, separation of the executive, legislature and judiciary, impracticability of amending the Constitution, etc, and little about the details of the proposed Lok Pal. The government side made the plea for excluding the Prime Minister from the purview of the Lokpal on the ground that the office of P.M. is the pivot of the parliamentary system. This was interestingly rebutted by Santosh Hegde of Anna's team by referring to the existing legal position. The Prevention of Corruption Act did not exclude the Prime Minister from the category of public servant to be hauled up under it. Even a Sub-Inspector, Hegde added to emphasise his point, could investigate a corruption case and file charge-sheet against a Prime Minister under the existing Law.

The ministers repeatedly talked about the sanctity of the constitutional frame work which should not be tinkered with. This was rebutted by Shanti Bhushan of Anna's team. He pointed out that the idea was simply to create an independent institution of Lokpal on the lines of the Election Commission, the U.P.S.C. and Supreme court within the existing constitutional structure. The ministers also opposed the inclusion of judiciary and lower level functionaries of the executive in the jurisdiction of the Lokpal. Justice Santosh Hegde observed that if the Prime Minister, Judiciary and lower level government functionaries, were excluded from the operation area of the Lokpal, then the Lokpal will hardly have any functions.

Although the meetings were claimed to have been held in 'cordial' atmosphere, a certain degree of blame game between the two sides could not be avoided. For instance, in the seventh meeting held on 15 June 2011, Kapil Sibal and Arvind Kejriwal were involved in a wordy duel of sorts in an exchange of allegations, but Anna stepped in to put an end to it. As a genuine and sincere crusader for an effective Lokpal, he affirmed that the two sides were not separate but one in drafting a suitable Lokpal Bill. The series of meetings not only failed to produce an agreed Lokpal Bill Draft, but the entire exercise was reduced to a forum for scoring an extra debating point.

In the circumstances, Anna Hazare had no option but to resort to the only means he knew of making a recalcitrant political establishment take his anti- corruption crusade with the seriousness it deserved. That was going on a fast unto death. He had resorted to it earlier in his home state of Maharashtra with considerable success. On 9 August 2003, he sat on a fast unto death to demand action against some ministers of the state government charged with corruption. He ended his fast on 17 August 2003 only when the Chief Minister announced the formation of a one man commission of inquiry headed by a retired High Court Judge to probe the charges. As a result, two ministers indicted by the inquiry commission had to resign in March 2005.

To be fair to Anna Hazare, it must be said that he had allowed enough time to the government to formulate agreed draft of the proposed Bill. The period between April and August 2011 was good enough to complete this task. Instead of taking up the job in all seriousness, the ministers in the drafting committee wasted the time and opportunity indulging in fruitless argumentation with the civil society members. Apart from Anna Hazare, the people at large, who had been aroused to a high level of consciousness against corruption, were greatly disappointed by the failure of the effort. Anna himself felt frustrated. He had already proclaimed his decision to sit on a fast unto death from 16 August 2011 if an agreed Jan Lokpal Bill was not introduced in the Parliament monsoon session beginning first August. As the government gave no indication of doing so, his supporters started preparing for the big day - Anna's fast unto death. The die had been cast. It was now the government's turn to handle it as best as it could. It had much prior experience of handling or mis-handling the situation that could possibly arise through its encounter with Anna's earlier four day fast and Baba Ramdev's mid - night camp.

But if the decision - makers of the government, the so-called core committee or whoever - had taken any lesson from these, it was the wrong one. They went on faltering at every step, from one blunder to another, until they landed in a tremendous mess from which it was difficult to wriggle out without a huge loss of face. Anna wanted to sit on his fast unto death at Jantar Mantar where he had done it earlier in April, the usual spot for all kinds of 'dharna' by all manners of protesters in Delhi. He was refused permission. He chose to do it in J.P. Park. He was not allowed. Finally, they agreed upon Delhi's Ramalila ground, the nerve-center of protest rallies in the national capital, as the permissible venue for his proposed fast, as they did not want to be seen as stifling a peaceful protest. Running with the hare and hunting with the hound. Anna and his supporters accepted it gratefully. For they could not have asked for anything better from the point of view of wide public visibility.

Well before the dateline of Anna's fast - 16 August 2011- people's support for his movement was sweeping the country. It was expressed in diverse ways. For instance, Mumbai's famous 'dubbawalas' (lunch-box carriers), about four to five thousands strong - affirmed their support for Anna in a novel way. They declared that there would be no service on 16 August-the starting date of Anna's fast - to show their solidarity with Anna. It may be noted that about two lakhs (2,00,000) home made lunch packs are transported everyday across Mumbai by these 'dabbawalas'. That was just a sample of how the commonest of the common man was stirred by Anna's movement.

More concerned citizens were worried about the sustainability of an indefinite fast by the 74 year old man and risk to his life. Many hoped against hope that some solution could be found out to break the deadlock and avoid the eventuality. Will he stop short of actually embarking upon his fast at this stage of his life? Or will he not? Will the government find an escape route and relent before the zero hour? The conscious citizens were harried by such questions during the days preceding 16 August. But the callous government remained unmoved. On the other hand, it sought to put hurdles in his way by not letting his supporters set up a tent in the rainy weather at the venue of his proposed fast in Ramlila ground.

And worse - The police arrested Anna Hazare from the place he was camping in Delhi at around 4 a.m. on 16 August 2011, hours before he was scheduled to begin his indefinite fast. The whole operation was meticulously organised. He was produced before the concerned judicial magistrate who promptly remanded him to judicial custody. He was just as promptly dispatched to Delhi's Tihar Jail to co-exist with some famous or infamous celebrities charged with corruption who were lodged there. The entire operation was over before the country knew about it. But once the electronic media broke the news, the nation erupted like never before in India's recent history.

4

"A Million Mutinies"

What an eruption it turned out to be! Tens of thousands of people took to the streets throughout the length and breadth of the country as the day progressed on 16 August. Within hours of the news of his arrest breaking on the networks, spontaneous protests broke out from Delhi and Kanpur in the North to Bangalore and Kochi in the South and from Baroda in the West to Bhubaneswar in the East. People from all walks of life, the classes as well as the masses, took to the streets not only in the metros but also in smaller towns. The rains in North India did not deter the people coming out drenched in the streets nor did the heat deter them in the South. Social activist Medha Patekar led a protest demonstration at Mumbai in Azad Maidan with an impressive turnout. In Nagpur, an army of protesters took over the main round-about on the busy Nagpur-Jabalpur national highway and courted arrest. Further south, the city of Hyderabad bubbling with life on a normal day wore a deserted look. Similar was the situation in almost all towns and cities across the country.

There were demonstrations in Visakhapatnam, Vijaywada, Guntur, Prakasham and many other smaller towns of Andhra Pradesh. In Bangalore, Santosh Hegde, a member of Anna's team, led the protests at Freedom Park, while scores of people went on a fast in Mangalore, Mysore, Belgaum, Bijapur and Hubli in the rest of Karnataka. There were protests and demonstrations in Surat, Vadodara, Rajkot, Nadiad, Bhavnagar, etc., in Gujarat. In the east, over 200 protesters went on a fast at Kolkata in the heart of the city and raised slogans in support of a strong Lokpal Bill. Even the remote north - eastern town of Shillong, the capital of

Meghalayay, was touched by the Anna wave where the faculty and students of the North Eastern Hill University staged a demonstration condemning Anna's arrest.

In the Hindi heartland, lawyers boycotted work at Allahabad High Court, a protest march was taken out in Lucknow, students of Gorakhpur university staged a demonstration and Anna's supporters blocked roads in Barabanki district to register loud protests against his arrest. In Patna, large number of protesters including women, young boys and girls assembled at Kargil Chowk, the sacred venue of all such rallies and demonstrations in the capital of Bihar. Some of them went on an indefinite fast to register their protest.

Nearer Delhi, markets in several districts of Haryana were shut down and train movements were disrupted. In Chandigarh, lawyers, teachers and members of the intelligentsia joined the protests in large numbers. In neighbouring Rajasthan, thousands participated in fasts at Bikaner, Sriganganagar, Kota, Bhilwara and Bundi and protesters courted arrest in Jaipur and Ajmer. The national capital, of course, was the nerve center where the action was. Thousands come out to express solidarity with Anna and protest against his arrest. Over one thousand protesters were arrested by police in course of the day. Student idealists who have always been in the vanguards of such protests all over the world, more so in India, were aghast at the government's audacity in arresting the most authentic anti-corruption crusader known to them. Their elders of an earlier generation recalled with horror the ruling party's black deeds during the 'emergency' regime. They were reminded of how J.P., Morarji Desai, Chandrashekar and other prominent opposition leaders were woken up at midnight, arrested and sent to jail. Anna's early morning arrest at about 4 a.m. had a striking resemblance to the midnight arrest of opposition leaders during the dark days of the 'Emergency.' They cried, *"murder of democracy."*

The government was once again in a pit. The 'wise men' of the government had calculated that Anna's supporters would move for his release which would be allowed on condition that he should move out of Delhi for maintenance of peace and order. Ostensibly, he was arrested on the ground that his proposed fast at Delhi would disturb public order in the national capital. Such a presumption was palpably wrong because as a true Gandhian, Anna had instilled the message of non-violence and peaceful means in the thought and action of his supporters. This was amply proved by the remarkable fact that inspite of such a high pitch of popular anger, there was no untoward incident in the wake of his arrest any where in the country. But there was no move for his release from Anna's side. For Anna was made of different mettle. Instead of asking for his release, he began his fast unto death at the scheduled time on 16 August in Tihar Jail itself.

The government's well calibrated plan of shifting Anna out of Delhi as a pre-condition of his release went haywire. And the decibel of public anger against the government was rising hour by hour that Anna had to remain confined in jail. People's jubilation associated with Independence Day celebrations was over-shadowed by the outrage against Anna's arrest. The extensive media coverage through numerous T.V. channels kept the people all over the country informed about hour to hour developments in the war of attrition between Anna and the government. And they gave vent to the disgust and anger over Anna's arrest in diverse ways.

Sonia Nair, a housewife in Mumbai came out to demonstrate against Anna's arrest with hundreds of others in the center of the city by singing the national anthem. "It was much better" she said, "than sitting in front of my TV being concerned and angry. I wanted to act. It is time to stand up in support of Anna rather than sit at home." Ritika Dutta, a young political science student at Delhi University, was shocked by the arrest of Anna and his associates. She blurted out, "This can only happen in India. People who are fighting against corruption are to day behind bars with corrupt ministers." (Quoted in an article, "Anna Hazare : Anti-Corruption Activist's Arrest Sparks protests across India," by Jason Burke in *The Guardian* (UK). Similar was the reaction of common citizens in cities and towns all over India.

By the afternoon of 16 August, the situation was on the verge of explosion. The "wise men" of the government had not bargained for this. All their calculations and meticulous planning had gone wrong. Keeping a tab on the pulse of the people from hour to hour, they panicked. And in a dramatic reversal of their earlier stance, they decided to set Anna Hazare free without any strings attached.

It was now Anna's turn to pay them back for their misadventure. Even as the police asked the jail authorities to release him, he refused to come out of Tihar jail. He had already started his fast in the forenoon in the jail itself and decided to stay put inside the premises during the rest of the afternoon and night. In a queer twist of circumstances, the government which was doing every thing to prevent Anna from staging his fast in the center of Delhi was now anxiously waiting for his coming out of the jail premises to Ramlila ground. For it dawned up-on the decision makers, belatedly though, that Anna in jail was far more dangerous then Anna in Ramlila ground.

Even though taken out of the prison cell in which he was kept after his arrest, Anna continued with his fast in the jail premises through the night and early next morning. It was in the forenoon of 17 August that he shifted to the make-shift stage hastily prepared by his followers in the Ramlila ground which was to be his habitat for the next twelve days.

Much water flowed in the Yamuna during the twelve days that Anna fasted in Ramlila Maidan in the open view of thousands of people who gathered there and lakhs who saw the scene live in the their TV sets across the country. There were endless confabulations, discussions and strategic sessions among the concerned ministers themselves behind the scene. They also interacted with the Anna's team directly or though interlocutors. Prominent among them were Sri Sri Ravi Shankar and Bhaiyu Maharaj, Anna's spiritual friend. But all this direct and back- channel exercise failed to break the ice till the beginning of the second week of Anna's fast. With clenched fist, the fasting 74-year old crusader exhorted the crowds around him from his make-shift bed to fight it out peacefully and demonstrate in front of MPs' houses for supporting his Jan Lokpal Bill. The crowds readily responded.

A patently restrictive and damaging provision in the government Lokpal Bill drew sharp criticism from the Anna's team. It provides harsh penalties to those making 'false, frivolous or vexatious' complaint against any public servant. Such complainants, accordingly to the government's bill, would be penalised with two to five years imprisonment and a fine ranging from Rs. 25,000 to 2 lakh. And, hold your breath, prosecution of those making the complaint would be at the government's expense and the complainants would be liable to pay compensation to the public servant concerned, besides meeting the public servant's legal expenses in contesting the case. This draconian provision in the government Bill would largely discourage people from filling complaints against the corrupt. Anna and his team mocked this provision by loudly declaring that it was meant to protect the corrupt and punish those who complain against them. And the people readily agreed with their assessment in denouncing the government bill.

Popular anger at government's brinkmanship in talks with Anna's team was mounting, with serious concern about Anna's declining health parameters as the fast progressed. To add to the flame, some ruling party politicians started the usual game of mud slinging against the members of the Anna's team. Arvind Kejriwal and Kiran Bedi, two most vocal and active members of the team, were targeted by raising issues about the NGOs with which they were associated. And the cake was taken by a prominent Congress party spokesman who went to the extent of dubbing Anna himself as steeped in corruption. "Preposterous" was the instant reaction of people glued to the news channels. Thousands across the country who were keenly watching the developments from day to day were outraged. It is another matter that this "worthy" spokesman later apologised for his unsavoury remarks about Anna, but enough damage had been done by then to the image of the ruling party and the government in the public eye.

Another ruling party stalwart, well-known as a mouthpiece and apostle of all kinds of lost causes, repeatedly pronounced that Anna was playing in the hands of the Sangh (R.S.S.). His Sangh-phobia was so deep - that he saw the saffron hand of the Sangh in everything that was said and done against the ruling party and its government. So much so that people had come to dismiss his habitual outbursts with a shrug of their shoulders.

For opposition politicians of an earlier generation, it was like the "Emergency" period when the ruling party and its government saw the "foreign hand" in every protest against the regime. Even the effort to rake up the issue of Arvind Kejriwal's and Kiran Bedi's NGO trusts reminded people of the emergency regime digging into the records of some Gandhian institutions to fish out some irregularities in receipt of funds. It was like looking in a dark night for a black cat which was not there.

Some senior ministers also used harsh language and talked tough with the members of Anna's team - Arvind Kejriwal and Kiran Bedi - involved in the negotiations with the government. But the ruling party's and the ministers' smear campaign against Anna and his team badly boomeranged against themselves. The more they harangued against Anna and his team, the greater was the anger of the people against them, their party and the government. For in the eyes of the people, Anna had come to become India's face in the country's fight against corruption. No one in the thousands and lakhs who had rallied behind him was bothered about the contents and merits of the Lokpal Bills drafted by the two sides. Not even the crowds of discerning middle classes. For the crowds assembled in Delhi's maidan and TV viewers all over the country, it was a clash between the corrupt political establishment and those fighting against it, in which they were overwhelmingly with the latter.

In the process, the institution of Lokpal itself, its shape and size, scope and modalities receded into the background, if not forgotten altogether. In popular view, it boiled down to a straight clash between the bad and ugly and good and beautiful, between the evil and good, between black and white. There was no grey area any more and the people were hugely on the side of the white. A junior minister trying to present the government's case at Ranchi, the capital of Jharkhand, was booed and jeered. No one was prepared to listen to him.

Anna's declining health, being monitored from day to day basis, by a team led by Dr. Naresh Trehan, added to the tension in the air. Hundreds of anti-corruption army of crusaders were sitting on indefinite fast alongwith Anna in different cities and towns. The conditions of many of these unknown and unsung idealists were also deteriorating as days passed, but they were determined not to break their fast until Anna did it.

By the end of the 9th day of his fast, Anna's health parameters - blood pressure, pulse rate, heart rate - were touching the danger level. Continuation of the fast any further could prove to be risky according to the doctors led by Dr. Trehan, which was relayed by the news channels. Anna was seen lying down on his make shift bed in the Maidan visibly weakjsitting up, addressing the crowds for a moment and lying down. People all over the country watched the scene anxiously in their TV channels, keeping their fingers crossed. The old - timers were reminded of Mahatma Gandhi's 21-day fast in jail in February 1943 and the deep anxiety, anguish and tension it had aroused among the people. But that was under the British rule when people were in shackles.

This time round, the scene was being enacted in full view of a free people aroused to a high pitch over the fast undertaken by a Gandhian for a right cause. The protesting crowds all over the country of 120 million were seething with anger mixed with deep anxiety, which they were giving vent to in multiple ways. A 'million mutinies' indeed.

5

The Truce and the Impact

The groundswell of popular sentiment in favor of Anna and against the government had reached explosive proportions. The gravity of the situation was not lost on the government which could no longer afford to ignore it. The ruling party leadership got into the act with the urgency that the situation warranted. In fact, backchannel efforts had already begun earlier to persuade Anna to break his fast by yielding on minor points. But the fasting old man and his team were proving hard nuts to crack. It now dawned upon the government that stubbornness or feeble and half-baked solutions would not work to break the deadlock. It had to walk more than halfway to make the other side walk to cover the distance that separated them.

The political leadership got into the stride with the required speed. It went through the motions with the government's core group meetings, consultations, discussions and an all-party meeting in a damage control exercise. After 14 meetings between the government and Anna's team, the impasse was temporarily resolved. On August 27, 2011, both the Houses of Parliament passed "*Sense of the House*" Resolutions agreeing, in principle, on the following key issues: *Citizens' Charter, Lower Bureaucracy* also to be under the Lokpal through appropriate mechanism, and establishment of *Lokayuktas in the States.* Legally speaking, as Subhash Kashyap, former Lok Sabha Secretary General pointed out, the sense-of-the-house resolution was, at best, only an in-principle agreement with respect to three issues, which were merely "forwarded" to the Standing Committee rather than a firm commitment from the Parliament. But it was unprecedented because perhaps never before had the Parliament held a sitting on a holiday to discuss an issue raised by a non-political entity. It was history in the making as the Parliament conceded that people should be taken into account while drafting legislation. *(Frontline,* Sept. 23, 2011)

And on Sunday, 28 August, 2011, the 13th morning of his fast, Anna broke his high-profle fast by sipping coconut water. Thousands who had gathered at the venue of the fast to watch this happy moment burst into loud cheers. Lakhs of people across the country who were glued to the news channels went into wild celebrations. Looking tired but jubilant, Anna said that his movement has "created a faith that country can be rid of corruption."

The political establishment felt relieved as the stand-off came to an amicable end. The whole nation heaved a sigh of relief. Anna himself declared that it was the support of tens of thousands of people across the country which led to the success of his campaign for an effective anti-corruption law. People's Parliament, he proclaimed, was bigger than Delhi's Parliament. The national media widely hailed it as "people's victory."

The international media did not lag behind in eulogizing Anna and his campaign. Reporting from Delhi, Dean Nelson wrote in *The Telegraph,* UK, dated 21 August, 2011, "Mr Hazare, a 74-year old 'Gandhian' social activist, has won widespread support throughout the country for his indefinite fast for stronger anti-corruption laws and captured the country's heart with his simple white homespun pyjamas and Gandhi cap or topi." Some reporters in foreign media hailed him as the new 'Gandhi' out to eradicate widespread corruption in India. Paul de Bendern of the news agency, *Reuters,* wrote on 28 August, 2011, the day Anna broke his fast: "Hazare rallied millions of predominantly urban middle class, angry at the government's inability to crack down on rampant corruption, made evident by the arrest of a minister and the poor state of infrastructure and services in a country that has grown at around 8 per cent per annum over the last few years."

The most significant impact of Anna's anti-corruption movement was felt in neighbouring Pakistan. Social activists in that country hailed Anna's crusade against corruption and wanted something like that to happen in Pakistan also which was similarly afflicted with the scourge of corruption. In pursuance of this, a three-member Pakistani delegation met Anna Hazare at his home village, Ralegan Siddhi, on 21 September, 2011. The delegation consisted of former Pakistan law minister, Iqbal Haider, former Pakistan Supreme Court judge, Nasir Ahmed Zahid and trade-unionist Karamat Ali. They invited Anna to visit Pakistan to initiate a movement similar to the one he had launched in India. The delegation informed Anna that a Pakistani social activist, Raja Jehangir Akhtar, was on hunger strike in Islamabad since 12 September seeking an anti-corruption legislation in Pakistan.

At the end of the meeting, Justice Zahid told reporters: "Hazare's movement has become a topic of great significance in Pakistan and other countries of the world. On behalf of the people of Pakistan, we congratulate him. We invited him to visit Pakistan and he has accepted it." The Pakistani delegation urged Anna not to limit his anti-corruption crusade to India, but to extend it all over South Asia. Anna agreed and emphasised that the success of his movement in India was mainly due to the ideals of Mahatma Gandhi. (*The Times of India,* Patna edn, 22 Sept,. 2011).

The impact of Anna's movement in neighbouring Pakistan was not surprising. In this age of information revolution and instant communication, borders between countries have been obliterated. This has been amply demonstrated in recent times in the countries of the Middle East. Regime change in Tunisia in response to people's uprising was followed by violent upheaval in Egypt resulting in the ouster of Hosni Mubarak after nearly four decades of absolute rule. In a chain reaction of sorts, Col Muammar Gaddafi's strongly entrenched regime in Libya was overthrown after a violent and bloody uprising of the people groaning under Gaddafi's dictatorship for decades. And the tremors of Egypt were felt in Yemen and Syria. In fact the whole of middle-east was on a boil threatening established regimes.

No wonder that Anna's anti-corruption storm starting in April 2011, which turned into a typhoon by August end, though non-violent and peaceful in the Gandhian tradition, had its ripples in Pakistan also. But that is part of a different story. The raging and tearing anti-corruption tornado had a far greater impact on India's own political establishment. In spite of the remarkable economic growth story - around 7 p.c. plus - under the leadership of an eminent economist Prime Minister, the Indian government appeared like a rudderless ship drifting along without a sense of direction for quite sometime. Absence of a strong and determinate political leadership was taking its toll on the functioning of the government. No one really knew where the power actually lay - in the Prime Minister or the shadowy Congress party leadership. In such a scenario, decision making in dealing with the situation arising out of the anti-corruption agitation became the first casualty. This showed in the flop show of the government in its encounter with the anti-corruption stir that shook the government and cast a shadow on its functioning. That was the immediate impact of Anna's movement on the internal political scenario which outweighed its impact beyond the borders of India.

Even before the Anna movement got into stride, the government had landed itself into a mess on the issue of 2G spectrum allotment scam. When the CAG report exposed the scam, a senior minister, who figured prominently in negotiations about Lokpal bill, brazen-facedly dismissed the CAG report as incorrect. He categorically asserted that the CAG calculation about loss of government revenue was wrong. He went to the extent of claiming that government had actually gained from the 2G spectrum allotments made by the then telecom minister. His tall claim was busted when the CBI registered a case under the Prevention of Corruption Act against the concerned minister and his cohorts. The minister was not only made to resign from the cabinet but also landed in jail. That was a sample of the incoherent and disjointed functioning of the government.

If that was so earlier, the government's interface with Anna's stir exposed its wavering and tottering character before the public. The anti-corruption movement which started as a citizens' protest in April grew into a peaceful people's uprising against the UPA government by the end of August 2011, thanks to the government's mishandling of the situation. Blowing hot and cold alternately, acting tough, climbing down and flexing muscles again had been the hallmark of government's interaction with the Anna movement.

To recapitulate the sequence of events, Anna'a simple demand in April was to bring up a strong Lokpal bill in consultation with his team of civil society activists. The government firmly rejected it claiming that framing of any legislation was the exclusive prerogative of Parliament. Anna sat on a fast at Jantar Mantar in protest and the whole country rallied behind him. After four days, the government yielded and agreed to the constitution of a joint drafting committee, including Anna and his team of civil society activists, to bring upon an agreed lokpal bill draft. Anna broke his fast on the 5th day. From mid-April to mid-August, government failed to produce an agreed draft after which Anna sat on a high profile fast in Ramlila ground with effect from 16 August against government's inflexible stand. The whole country rose in support of Anna. The joint drafting committee meetings were reduced to a farce, with the ruling party ministers' dismissive of Anna's team and peoples' power. And towards the last week of August, with people's anger reaching explosive proportions and government neck-deep in water, it came down from its high pedestal and conceded some of the key demands of Anna. As the government climbed down from the precipice, Anna broke his 12 grueling days' fast to the great relief of the nation and respite of the government.

It would be evident from the sequence of events narrated above that the government was seized with kind of a schizophrenia or split personality in dealing with Anna's agitation right from the start. At some crucial moments in course of the movement, it appeared struck up with paralysis. When the government leaders sought to counter Anna's case aggressively by mouthing high-sounding shibboleths and platitudes about parliamentary democracy, they placed themselves virtually in an adversary relationship with anti-corruption crusaders. In popular view, they appeared to be fighting those who were fighting against corruption. Nothing could be more damaging to the image and standing of a political party and its government in a democracy.

As noted earlier, some ruling party stalwarts vainly tried to tarnish the image of Anna and his team of social activists by digging into their antecedents. The more they did so, the more they and their party went down in popular estimation. The government's antics appeared more like the theatre of the absurd being enacted by its ministers in the corridors of power than aimed at addressing people's deep concern about corruption aroused by the little man from Ralegan Siddhi. And this blotted the credibility of the ruling party and its government as never before in such a short time. Commenting on the monsoon session of the parliament, the leader of the opposition in the Rajya Sabha said: "I have not seen the government lose its credibility in one single session of Parliament." (*The Times of India,* Patna edition, 10 Sept. 2011).

The report of a foreign agency which surveyed and quantified the political fall-out of Anna's agitation and the government's encounter with it was more specific. It said that before the start of Anna's movement, the stock of the ruling political party was well above the halfway mark and that of the principal opposition party (BJP) well below it. But at the end of the movement, the position was reversed. That is, at the end of August 2011, the principal opposition party's stock rose above the halfway mark and that of the ruling party slid down below the mark in the same proportion.

A September report of the US Congressional Service (CRS), a bipartisan and independent research wing of the US Congress which provides briefs for American legislators, said that the decline in the ruling Congress party's standing in recent months was 'precipitous.' It boldly projected the resurgence of the principal opposition party - the BJP - at the cost of the ruling party. (*The Times of India,* Patna edition, 15 Sept. 2011).

Such assessments of foreign agencies may or may not be correct but the fact remains that the anti-corruption tornado that hit the country had left the ruling political party badly scarred and bruised. Never before in recent times had so much damage been done to the image and credibility of an incumbent government in such a short span of four months from April to August 2011.

Leaving aside the debate on the issue of its political fall-out, the real impact of Anna's four month long crusade was to arouse the classes as well as masses to call for the installation of a strong Lokpal. To add to the voice of common masses, an elite group of topmost industrialists and economists of India sent an 'open letter' to the political leadership supporting the need for the urgent passage of a well-crafted lokpal bill by the Parliament. The signatories of the open letter included Ashok Ganguly, Azim Premji, Deepak Parikh, Jamshed Godrej, Anu Aga, Bimal Jalan and Keshub Mahindra. Even the Prime Minister, maintaining a stoic aloofness from his ministers' encounter with Anna from day to day, said in Parliament in the last week of August: "I applaud Anna, I salute Anna. I request all to tell Anna that his point has been registered and we will take note of it" (*Outlook,* 5 Sept, 2011). That said it all. A small town topiwala crusader hailing from Relegon Siddhi had woken up a sleeping nation to the urgent need for an Ombudsman to minimise, if not eliminate altogether, the cancer of corruption eating into the vitals of the country's progress. That was the true significance and impact of Anna's four-month long movement.

6

Background of Anti-corruption Legislation in India

The beginning of Anti-corruption legislation in India can be traced back to the enactment of the Indian Panel Code (IPC) by the colonial regime in 1860 which defined corruption as a crime punishable by law. The anti-corruption provisions incorporated in the IPC were meant to cover various categories of government employees *broadly* designated "Public Servants". It was a small beginning aimed at tackling endemic bribery and corruption of petty government servants at the cutting edge level.

The corruption scenario in the country remained more or less unchanged till the out-break of the second world war in 1939. Large scale purchases made by government departments in pursuance of the British war efforts and scarcity of essential commodities necessitated controls and rationing. This led to a quantum jump in corruption on the part of government functionaries including those of the middle and higher levels, 'It was to tackle this employees' corruption spectrum that the next stage was reached in the anti-corruption legislation. In early 1947 just before Independence, the colonial regime enacted the Prevention of corruption Act targeted against government and semi-government employees of all categories dubbed as "Public servant". Till then the incidence of corruption among politicians, who were just beginning to taste power as during the days of the provincial autonomy (1937-39) was negligible.

However, traces of corruption of politicians in power started showing during 28 months of congress party rule in several provinces under the scheme of Provincial Autonomy between 1937 and 1939. In comparison to what is seen today, "those would appear like tiny dots on a clean white sheet of probity in politicians" work and conduct. But in the Gandhian era of high standard of political morality, even those tiny dots caused grave concern to the Father of the nation. The Mahatma was gravely concerned about growing corruption in congress ranks and lashed out at it in his journal "Harijan". So much so that in May 1939 he told the Gandhi Seva Sangh workers, "I would go to the length of giving the whole congress organization a decent burial rather than put up with the corruption that is rampart". Mahatma Gandhi was much relieved when the congress ministries resigned in October 1939 on political issue arising out of Britain's entry in the Second World war in September. But those were different times when purity and cleanliness difined practising politics.

After the Mahatma his legacy of moral values, transparency and probity in public life was carried forward by Nehru almost single handed for Seventeen long years. There were rumblings of corruption in the corridors of power during his long tenure but he stuck to the narrow and straight path and acted to stomp it out. Interestingly, the first major case of financial irregularity involving a government undertaking was brought to light through a speech in parliament by Nahru's own son-in-law Feroze Gandhi. It related to purchase of shares of certain companies under the control of a business tycoon Haridas Mundhra by LIC in dubious circumstances in June, 1957. Mundhra was an industrial upstart who had emerged as a big businessman through hectic speculation and manupulations in shares.

When the Mundhra scams struck parliment and raised a storm, with Feroze Gandhi in the vanguard of the critics, the Finance Ministry which was the parent department of LIC came under loud criticism. Nehru's confidant and trusted Finance Minister T.T. Krishnamachari, an eminent economic administrator in his own right, not only accepted the demand for a public enquiry, but opted for a full fledged judicial enquiry. Thus a commission of enquiry headed by M.C. Chagla, then the Chief Justice of Bombay High Court, was set up in 1958 which enquired into the whole affair.

The Chagla commission found irregularities in the purchase of Mundhra shares by the Life Insurance corporation (LIC) at the initiative of the Finance Secretary, The Finance Minister personally was not involved in any way And yet, Justice Chagla observed. "In my opinion in any case, it is clear that constitutionally, the Minister is responsible for the action taken by his Secretary with regard to this transaction. It is clear that a Minister must take the responsibility for actions done by his subordinates. He cannot take shelter behind them, nor can he disown their action." The commission's report was enough to induce T.T. Khrishnamchari to resign, even though no stigma was attached to him personally. And Nehru accepted his resignation against his own best judgement about Krishnamachari's integrity and competence.

Another case of Ministerial lapse of a different kind involved K.D. Malvia, Minister of State for Mines and Fuel. There were allegations that he had received a gift of Rupees ten thousand from one Serajuddin of a company of Orissa which had dealings with his Ministry. A minister with known leftist leanings, he had done a lot to bring the Oil industry largely in the public sector and was ideologically close to Nehru. Yet when the allegations surfaced, Nehru had no hesitation in instituting an enquiry by justice S.K. Das, a retiring Judge of the Supreme Court. The enquiry commission faulted Malvia on two counts and that was the end of Malvia's political career. He resigned and his resignation was promptly accepted by Nehru.

In comparison to the present corruption scenario, these stray cases involving those in power were peanuts. But in the standards of uprightness of the Nehru era, these were enough to induce the leaders of the country to address the problem of corruption seriously. Accordingly, a committee on prevention of corruption was set up for the first time in independent India under the Chairmanship of K. Santhanam in 1962 to suggest remedial measures. The terms of reference of this committee however was limited to consider primarily the problem of corruption among "public servants" which was then supposed to mean only government employees. It was only incidentally that the committee went in to the issue of Ministerial Corruption as part of corruption in Administration in general. The Committee submitted its report on 31st March, 1964 touching upon the issue of Ministerial corruption. And the simplistic remedy it recommended to tackle it was to include Ministers also in the definition of 'public servants' liable under the provisions of the anti- corruption laws already in place. Initially, the Government was not inclined to accept this part of Santhanam Committee's recommendations on the ground that Ministers were not mere 'public servants' but had a greater moral and social responsibility towards the people. There was some justification in the initial reaction of the Government against clubbing the Ministers with the common category of Government employees in terms of the anti-corruption laws. For most of those who occupied Ministerial positions in early post independence years were products of the freedom movement. They were supposed to be not only above board themselves but also leading the people on the path of uprightness. When some among them or their successors fell from the high pedestal to the mire of corrupt ways, the political system not really prepared for it, was taken by surprise.

In any case, the issue of Ministers' inclusion in the category of 'public servants' for coverage under anti-corruption laws had already been settled by the Supreme Court. In a landmark judgement, the Supreme Court had included Ministers in the definition of 'public servants.' Inclusion of Ministers and Chief Ministers in the list of 'Public servants' coming within the purview of anti-corruption laws is an accepted fact and settled law now. There still remained a grey area regarding members of Parliament and State Legislatures in this respect. This was remedied by the enactment of a more comprehensive Prevention of Corruption Act in 1988. This Act so widened the scope of the term 'public servant' as to include lawmakers also.

7

History of Lokpal Bills that were Aborted

Even before the Santhanam Committee Submitted its report in March 1964, the idea of constituting the institution of Lokpal was first mooted in 1963 during a debate on demands for grants of the law Ministry of Government of India. Evidently, the basic idea of Lokpal was borrowed from the institution of Ombudsman in existence in western countries like Sweden, Denmark, Norway, Finland and several others. These will be dealt with at some length later in another chapter. The next stage in the evolution of the *concept of Lokpal was reached in 1966 when the first* Administrative Reforms Commission recommended that two independent authorities at the Central and State levels should be established to enquire into complaints against public functionaries including Members of Parliament. Accordingly a Lokpal Bill was introduced in Parliament for the first time in 1968. But it lapsed with the dissolution of the Lok Sabha.

The very next year in 1969, P.K. Deo, a Swatantra Party M.P. from Orissa, made a strong plea for creating the institution of Lokpal in accordance with the recommendation of the Administrative Reforms Commission headed by Morarji Desai. After a lively debate on the issue, the Government introduced a Bill in Parliament in August 1969. Moving the Bill on 13th August, 1969, the Minister of State for Home Affairs Observed. "This Bill to create an institution of Lokpal and Lokayukts has been brought forward in view of the public demand to create an institution to look after grievances and allegations which are made from time to time by the members of the public against the administration",

(Quoted in the book "Lokpal: facts and Arguments" by P. Venkateswar Rao Jr., Published by Har Anand Publications Pvt. Ltd.) The Bill was passed in the Lok Sabha on 20 August, 1969. But, as it happened repeatedly since then, it did not go through the Rajya Sabha and lapsed when elections were called in 1971 Incidentally, it was the only time a Lokpal Bill had reached that stage in the past.

Since August, 1969 when the First Lokpal Bill was passed by Lok Sabha and was allowed to lapse, the Lokpal issue remained hybernating in cold storage for full 42 years until it was raised in a big way by Anna Hazare in August, 2011. And that when at least two important Commissions made specific recommendations for creating the institution of Lokpal during the period. In 2002 the National Commission to review the working of the constitution urged that the constitution should provide for the appointment of Lokpal at the center and Lokayuktas in states. The Second Administrative Refporms Commission, formed in 2005, also recommended that the office of Lokpal be established without delay. Even the U.P.A. Government's National Common Minimum Programme promised in 2004 to enact a Lokpal Bill.

And yet, the non-enactment of a Lokpal Bill for 42 long years since its first aborted introduction in parliament in 1968 speaks volumes about the apathy and indifference of the political establishment towards the institution of Lokpal. Successive governments at the center though made a show of acting on the Lokpal front, only to allow it to turn into a no-show.They went through the motions all right of bringing up Lokpal Bill in parliaments with monotonous regularity to keep up their image before the public without letting it pass into the Statute book. In the process, Lokpal Bill was introduced in the Lok Sabha eight more times after 1968, that is, in 1971, 1977, 1985, 1989, 1996, 1998, 1999 and 2001 without becoming a law, each time the bill was allowed to lapse except in 1985 when it was officially withdrawn. That tells its own story about the unwillingness of politicians in power to set up an ombudsman type watchdog over themselves.

That probably would be a record of sorts about a proposed

bill dragging along for over four decades without being passed by parliament in India or in any other Country of the world. The chequered history of Lokpal bill that failed to made it to the Statute book for so long added to the legitimacy and urgency of Anna's movement in the eyes of the people. Justice Santosh Hegde of Anna's team once remarked in August 2011 that if the government had the will, Lokpal Bill could be passed in a matter of days. The people readily agreed and that raised the tempo and the anger of the vast middle classes in the vanguard of the agitation against the government.

Even the ritual of bringing a Lokpal Bill before parliament and then allowing it to lapse had stopped for nearly a decade when Anna revived the issue. The last time that a Lokpal Bill was introduced in parliament was in 2001 when the National Democratic Alliance Government was in power. It may be noted that the government then in power moved three Bills for establishment of Lokpal within a period of years - 1998, 1999 and 2001. The United Progressive Alliance government led by Prime Minister Manmohan Singh, on coming to power in 2004, also promised to enact a Lokpal Bill in its Common Minimum Programme but failed to actually bring it up during its first term. It was one year after coming to power in Its Second term that the U.P.A., Shaken by various mega scams surfacing in the country, recalled its commitment to bring up a Lokpal Bill. Accordingly, the government prepared an official Lokpal Bill in 2010 for the first time after 2001.

Even this Bill was only drafted showing the intention of the government, like a memo of intent, and not actually introduced in parliament by the time Anna's movement began in April, 2011. As such, it can be clubbed together with the other aborted Bills as the last of the series. However, since it was the base point from which subsequently the government started negotiations with Anna's team, it would be relevant here to touch upon it briefly.

In the 2010 government's draft, the Lokpal was to consist of a chairperson and two members, each one to be either a retired Judge of the Supreme Court or the Chief Justice of a High Court. They were to be selected by a Committee headed by the vice

President of India and comprising the Prime Minister, speaker of the Lok Sabha, Home Minister, Law Minister, Leader of the opposition in Lok Sabha and Leader of the opposition in Rajya Sabha. The Lokpal so constituted could be removed by the President of India after an enquiry by the Supreme Court into any Complaint against the organisation.

To begin with, the very process of selection of Lokpal proposed in the Bill was so heavily weighted in favour of the ruling political party or the government in power as to make it virtually a department of the incumbent government rather than a watchdog over it. For out of seven members of the Selection committee, five would actually be ruling party nominees and only two belonging to the opposition with no independent Civil Society Member. The Prime Minister, Home Minister and Law Minister are direct members of the government and vice president and Speaker are nominees of the ruling party in our political system. What kind of watchdog function could be expected from such a Lokpal, if members of the ruling party and its government were themselves charged with corruption?

How such a government dominated selection panel could go astray was amply illustrated in the appointment of Central Vigilance Commissioner by the Central government. An I.A.S. officer facing corruption charges himself in the state of his parent cadre was made the C.V.C by a selection committee comprising the Prime Minister, Home Minister and the Leader of the apposition in Lok Sabha. And this, inspite of the objection to his selection made by the leader of the opposition. When questions were raised against this appointment, the government first justified the appointment and when roundly cornered on the choice of a scam-tainted person as the anti-corruption watchdog, as C.V.C. is supposed to be, the government came out with the fantastic plea that the record of the selected officer about his facing corruption charges in his parent state was not placed before the Selection Committee. But there was no answer to the point that the appointment was made inspite of objection raised by the Leader of the opposition. It was ultimately left for the Supreme Court to cancel the appointment of the incumbent Central Vigilance Commissioner.

That is not to cast any aspersion or pass Judgment on the integrity of the concerned officer. The charges against him might or might not be proved. The important point to note here is that, in absence of a comprehensive institution of Lokpal, the Central Vigilance Commissioner is the only statutory functionary to keep an eye on corruption in higher bureaucracy even though in an advisory capacity. And such an anti-corruption functionary must be himself or herself absolutely above suspicion like ceaser's wife. If that could happen in appointment of a Central Vigilance Commissioner by a government-dominated selection Committee, how could the appointment of a Lokpal by such a Committee be considered valid and trustworthy?

Leaving aside the faulty selection process, the Lokpal as envisaged in the government's draft Bill of 2010 was so hedged in by saving clauses as to render it virtually toothless in dealing with politicians' corruption. For instance, the Lokpal could not enquire into any allegation of corruption against the Prime Minister in so far as it related to national security, maintenance of public order, national defences and foreign relations. This could be justified to an extent, but the saving clause in regard to members of parliament was absolutely crippling. For the Lokpal could not enquire into any allegation of corruption against any M.P. without the recommendation of the speaker of Lok Sabha or Chairman of Rajya Sabha as the case may be.

Further although any member of the public other than a public servant could lodge a complaint before the Lokpal, but here again it had to be routed through the Presiding officer of the concerned House of Parliament. That is, such a public complaint against ministers and members of either House of parliament had to be made to the Speaker of the Lok Sabha or Chairman of the Rajya Sabha, as the case may be, and not directly to the Lokpal. Only those complaints against the above category of politicians could be entertained by the Lokpal which were referred to it by the speaker of the Lok Sabha or the Chairman of the Rajya Sabha.

As if that was not enough, the government Lokpal Bill of 2010 provided that the Lokpal shall not enquire into any matter or person if the chairman or any member had bias, regarding the person or matter. In case of such a bias, the person complained against could apply to the President of India who would obtain the opinion of the Chief Justice of India to decide if the Lokpal could enquire or not. In simple terms, if the person to be enquired into by Lokpal petitioned the President of India about bias, the Chairman or the concerned member of Lokpal would himself be under scrutiny by the Chief Justice of India. Apart from reducing the institution of Lokpal to nothingness, this proviso verges on absurdity. If the Government's Lokpal Bill of 2010 was an expression of intent, it showed that the government intended to create a farce in the name of Lokpal. No crusader for Lokpal to Curb Corruption could take it. Certainly not the inspired team of Anna Hazare.

In any case, even this mockery of a Lokpal Bill was not introduced by government in parliament till April 2011 when Anna launched his campaign. That changed the plot of the story of Lokpal completely. What followed has been comprehensively dealt with in earlier chapters. The government's Lok pal Bill 2010 was consigned to the records of the government as the last of the series of aborted Lokpal Bills which never came up.

The shape and content of the Jan Lokpal Bill brought up by Anna's civil society team and the official Lokpal Bill drafted by the government shall be dealt with a little later. But before that a peep into the corruption situation in post-independence India and sporadic efforts to curb it from time to time is necessary. In the early post-independence years, the situation was well under check as long as Nehru was around at the helm as the standard-bearer of the nation. The slide down started after the great helmsman departed from the scene. It would, therefore, be worth while to glance through the beginnings of corruption on the part of politicians in power or ministers misconduct in post. Nehru era. The plethora of corruption scandals that rocked the country since then would provide a fitting backdrop to the Lokpal movement and explain why it started at the time it did.

8

Beginnings of Ministers Misconduct

Laws and institutions of governance are products of a nation's endeavors to meet the challenges it is faced with from time to time. They are entirely need based and keep changing in keeping with the requirements of social good, except for those incorporating some external verities which are valid for all times. This is true of laws and institutions meant for promoting clean and corruption-free political dispensation as in other spheres of social life. That is, if there is a sea change in the scale and dimension of corruption in the socio-political life of the country, the laws and institutions meant to counter it also need to be changed accordingly.

When, for instance, there was a quantum jump in corruption on the part of government employees in India during and after the Second World War, the landmark Prevention of Corruption Act as enacted in 1947 which became the bedrock of anti-corruption effort of the government. (And when some improvements upon the 1947 Act were needed, a fresh and revised anti-corruption act was brought about in 1988). A Special Police Unit, now famous as CBI, was also created to investigate and prosecute cases of corruption among central government employees by enacting the Delhi Special Police Establishment Act in 1946.

Those were the times when corruption itself was largely confined to government employees, termed as "public servants" and necessary legal and institutional framework was provided to deal with that. Incidence of corruption among politicians, who were only beginning to taste power, was negligible. And whenever any flame of corruption, however minor, touched a politician in power, Nehru readily doused it by prompt action. As discussed in earlier chapter, T.T. Krishnamachari, the impeccable Finance Minister and K.D. Malviya, Minister of State, had to quit when splinters of Mundhra and another scam just touched them.

Nehru upheld the Gandhian legacy of uprightness in public life till his last hour. During the closing years of his life, allegations of corruption started surfacing against Sardar Pratap Singh Kairon, the redoubtable Chief Minister of Punjab. These were primarily directed against his sons and relatives supposed to be exploiting their kinship ties to promote their material interests. Pratap Singh Kairon, it may be noted, was doing pioneering work to take Punjab out of the trauma of partition on to the path of economic miracle. He is still regarded as the maker of modern Punjab. And yet Nehru, after initial hesitation, decided to institute a judicial enquiry against Kairon. Accordingly, a commission of enquiry headed by S.R. Das, a former Chief Justice of India, was set up in November 1963. That was his last act to uphold the high standard of probity in public life, for he survived hardly for six months after the institution of enquiry. Incidentally, it was the first and unique case of a judicial enquiry on charges of corruption set up against a Chief Minister in office by the Government of India.

The legacy of Nehru was carried forward by the 'little' great man Lal Bahadur Shastri, an epitome of simplicity and honesty himself. The S.R. Das Commission submitted its report on 11 June 1964, just three days after Lal Bahadur Shastri took over as Prime Minister. The enquiry commission concluded as follows: "The commission is free to conclude that a father cannot legally or morally prevent his sons from carrying on business, but the exploitation of the influence of the father, who happens to be the Chief Minister of the state, cannot be permitted to be made a business of...........There is no getting away from the fact that Pratap Singh Kairon knew or had more than ample reason to think or suspect that his sons or relatives were allegedly exploiting his influence and powers."

A scrutiny of the report would clearly indicate that Pratap Singh was personally not involved in any way in the business affairs of his sons and relatives. The commission only presumed that he could not have been unaware of these business activities. And yet Lal Bahadur Shastri saw to it that Pratap Singh Kairon resigned. Kairon's initial reaction was to stick to his office as no personal irregularity or wrongdoing was found against him. But when Shastri got the report published, Kairon had no option but to quit. Incidentally, if such a strict criterion is followed now, many ministers will have to go Kairon's way and quit office.

As long as stalwarts of freedom movement like Nehru and Shastri were at the helm of political establishment, no one thought of an ombudsman or lokpal. The top leadership of the country was good enough and believed to be so as to prevent the wielders of power from straying off the straight path. It was no mere coincidence that the First Administrative Reforms Commission headed by Morarji Desai recommended for the first time the creation of an independent authority to enquire into complaints against public functionaries including members of Parliament in 1966 and that the first aborted Lokpal Bill was introduced in Parliament in 1968. In reality, that signified the end of the Gandhian legacy of clean public life unsullied by the pollution of corruption.

At this stage, corruption of ministers at State level started coming to light. There were a few judicial enquiry commissions against Chief Ministers of some States (Bihar and Orissa) and their ministerial colleagues. These were set up by the successor governments of states concerned and none by the Government of India as in the case of Kairon.

The canker of corruption, which went on spreading its fangs, was more visible at State level. Since most of the States were ruled by the Congress party, the state of affairs was best commented by two straight-forward Chief Ministers of the ruling party itself. In October 1972, Siddharta Shankar Ray of West Bengal said at the AICC session: "As a chief minister of only six months experience, I have no hesitation in saying that none of our politics will succeed unless we are substantially able to eradicate corruption." P.C. Sethi, the chief minister of Madhya Pradesh, was more candid. He said: "Everyone wants to grab money in whatever way he can. If somebody becomes a chief minister, he wants to make fortune not only for himself but for three or four generations to come." That said it all.

The practice of allotting "paying" portfolios to trusted ministers and sharing in the "profits" was being increasingly adopted by chief ministers of states. The powder-keg of public anger against mounting corruption at the state level first erupted in Gujarat in early 1974. A raging and tearing youth agitation started in Gujarat against what was alleged to be collection of funds for financing the ruling Congress party campaign in UP election in 1974. In this dubious exercise, it was widely believed, the line between party chest and personal pile was totally obliterated. The *Nav Nirman* agitation, as it was called, was launched and conducted entirely by students fired by idealism to usher in a corruption-free society. And its undisguised target was ministers' corruption.

The Nav Nirman movement agitation started in Gujarat and gradually snowballed into a much wider movement leading to turbulent political developments that followed. The spontaneous youth revolt against political corruption in Gujarat aroused a sleeping giant and one of the titans of the freedom struggle - Jay Prakash Narayan. After quitting formal politics and joining Vinobha Bhave's *Bhoodan* movement in June 1954, JP had confined himself to multiple nation- building and humanitarian missions in different parts of the country. At the time of Gujarat students' agitation, he was engaged in dousing the fire of sporadic naxalite movement in North Bihar countryside. The raging idealism of Gujarat students stirred his imagination and revived his latent activism against political ills of the country of which corruption was a basic part. In his own Bihar too, students were on a boil against various genuine and imaginary grievances largely focused on political corruption. They forced a violent confrontation with the government right in front of the state secretariat on 18 March 1974. When the law enforcement agencies came down heavily to suppress them, the agitating students placed themselves at the command of J.P. to fight against political corruption.

JP saw in this his last chance to bring about revolutionary social and political changes through youth activism. He encapsulated all his ideas of desired change in what he called *Total*

Revolution. It incorporated everything from land redistribution, decentralization of power, right to recall of elected representatives to abolition of caste and dowry systems, besides, of course, political corruption. Thus, what had started as a youth protest against rampant political corruption in Gujarat turned into a rambling and Utopian "total revolution" in the hands of JP.

JP's total revolution remained a failed Utopia but started a chain of momentous events that shook the country. What followed is recent history. Imposition of the infamous *Emergency* in June 1975, the absolutist rule of the Congress party for two and a half years, the overthrow of the Grand Old Party from power at the center in March 1977 after 30 years of uninterrupted rule, the interregnum of Janata party rule and finally return of the GOP to power in 1980 are well-known facts. The growing incidence of corruption on the part of power-wielders was over-shadowed by the turbulent political developments during this period. The issue of corruption was dwarfed by the threat to the democratic system itself in the wake of the "emergency" and the misdeeds of the emergency regime.

It is no wonder that the idea of Lokpal as a watchdog against corruption remained in a state of animated suspension for six years between 1971 and 1977. The Janata government headed by Morarji Desai did introduce it in 1977, but it failed to come off as the Janata dispensation itself came to an end before the end of 1979. The restoration of the Congress party regime in 1980 was followed by another devastating turmoil related to secessionist movement in Punjab, the *operation bluestar* and the raging violence in its wake, culminating in the tragic assassination of Prime Minister Indira Gandhi on 31st October 1984. The whole nation remained on tenterhook until restoration of peace and installation of Rajiv Gandhi as Prime Minister. A lokpal bill was reintroduced by Rajiv Gandhi's government in 1985 only to be withdrawn subsequently. That heralded the beginning of a fresh wave of corruption scandals dealt with in the next chapter.

9

Scam After Scam

The corruption scandals that erupted after mid 1980 involving the high and the mighty were so vast that volumes could be filled dwelling upon them. Once the flood gates were opened, there was no stopping the torrent of scams sweeping across the country in waves after waves. It would need a whole book to cover all such scams at some length which is beyond the scope of this chapter. What is attempted here is only to touch upon some of the well known scams that surfaced towards the end years of the 20th century. These are as follows :

Bofors Gun Deal Scam

Hardly had the embers of Indira Gandhi's tragic assassination dimmed when the Bofors Gun deal scandal exploded in 1987. It related to 285 million dollars contract with the Swedish arms company, Bofors for supply of 155 mm Howitzer Guns. It came into light that A.B. Bofors paid huge amounts of kickbacks to Indian authorities concerned for winning the bid for supply of these guns. The disclosure came from Norway where a radio channel broadcast the full story. Those accused of receiving the kickbacks included Hinduja Brothers, the N.R.I. business tycoons based in London, S.K. Bhatnagar, the incumbent Defence Secretary of India and above all Ottavio Quattrocchi, a high profile Italian business representative operating in India at that time.

Although the amount of the bribe alleged to have been paid was not too big, the scam hogged the limelight and badly scarred the image of the ruling political party in the eyes of the people. Sensing the public mood and taking advantage of the situation

V.P. Singh, the incumbent Finance Minister in Rajiv Gandhi's Government, resigned from the Government and the ruling party to project himself as a national hero out to fight corruption. He clubbed together a rag-tag political outfit comprising political parties then in wilderness to challenge the ruling Congress Party in the general election that followed. As a result, the ruling Congress Party which had won 421 seats in the previous Lok Sabha election got only 197 seats in the parliamentary election held in 1989. The Bofors scam thus had an oversize impact on the existing political establishment leading to the ouster of the ruling Congress Party from the seat of power.

Harshad Mehta Bank Scam

It related to illegal diversion of ONGC funds amounting to Rs. 650 crores through UCO Bank to the account of Harshad Mehta between July 1988 and March 1991 on payment of hefty bribes. Harshad Mehta used this money received on a platter, courtesy the corrupt officials of ONGC and UCO Bank, to play at high stakes in the stock and money markets. In one of the many cases taken up in this regard, the CBI submitted charge-sheet against Harshad Mehta, his brother Ashwin Mehta and two top officials of ONGC and UCO Bank in July 1996. This was only one of the shady transactions Harshad Mehta, with suspected political connections, indulged in.

Although Harshad Mehta swindled hundreds of crores of public money through manipulation of Banks and Stock Exchange operations, this corruption scandal did not have any big fall out on the fate of the Government or the Party in power. Except that two Ministers of Narshimha Rao Government B. Shankaran and Rameshwar Thakur had to quit because of some adverse findings in the scam.

Sugar Import Scandal

Even before Harshad Mehta's story of corruption could get stale, a sugar import scandal came to light in the autumn of 1994. By deliberately not opting to import sugar to meet domestic needs when prices in international market were relatively lower and importing large quantities at a higher price later, the government put the country to a loss of few hundred crores of rupees. And the loss of the government exchequer was the illegitimate gain of government functionaries concerned. Though relatively minor in nature, it kept the sleaze columns of newspapers busy and the chain of corruption stories popping up like a soar thumb. In the process, another notable Minister of Narsimha Rao's government, Kalpnath Rai who was handling the Sugar Portfolio had to quit office.

Jain Hawala Payment Scandal

One of the more sensational scandals of the last decade of the 20th century was what came to be known as Jain Hawala Scam. And the way it came to light was both interesting and intriguing. Interesting because it was just a chance detection which came about without any conscious effort and intriguing because the investigating agency kept it under the carpet for well over three years. It so happened that in course of a not much organised raid on hawala operators in Delhi in May 1991, the CBI stumbled upon and seized two diaries and two files from the residence of J.K. Jain, an employee of S.K. Jain of an industrial house based in Bhilai. The diaries contained names of a number of big politicians as recipients of hawala money which numbed the sleuths. It was like a hot potato for CBI top brass which they would have liked to keep under the carpet for as long as possible.

The CBI sat over the diaries for over three years on the pretext of deciphering the entries in the diaries and identifying the sources of hawala money. Meanwhile, two enterprising journalists Rajinder Puri and Vineet Narain filed public interest petition before the Supreme Court in October 1993. The petition urged the apex court to ask the CBI to expedite investigation into the Jain Hawala pay offs. It was on 29 November 1994 that the Supreme Court issued direction to the CBI to expedite investigation into the case and submit progress report for the court's scrutiny. From then onwards, the court kept prodding the CBI to "catch the big fish" and bring them for trial by courts of law.

In course of its continued pursuit of the matter, the Supreme Court expressed its exasperation at the slow pace of investigation from time to time. On 5 December 1994, the court made this telling observation : "if we are meant only to punish people of petty offences and let those who spend lakhs of rupees on birthday parties go scot-free, then we'd better close down the courts. It is difficult to believe that a thing so simple, which even a thanedar from a police station could solve, is beyond the CBI's caliber." In fact, any investigating agency under the control of the government of the day was likely to falter and hesitate to handle a scandal which could prove lethal for many members of that Government. That was the predicament of CBI in this case.

In the circumstances, it was entirely due to constant vigilance of the Supreme Court that CBI registered a regular case and completed the investigation against the accused persons including some Ministers of the Government in about a year after the court's stinging observation in December 1994 quoted above. Accordingly, the CBI sought the sanction of the President of India to prosecute three senior Cabinet Ministers on corruption charges in January 1996. And when on 16 January 1996, the CBI reported to the court about having sought Government's sanction to prosecute the Ministers, the court observed: "If there is any delay from any quarter in procuring permission, we shall intervene."

Without dwelling upon the protracted legal processes and end result of the case, it is enough to point out that CBI submitted charge-sheets for trial by court against over two dozen leading lights of India's political establishment of that period.

The Urea Import or Non-Import Scam

In November 1995, National Fertilizers Limited, a public sector company under the Ministry of Fertilizers, made full payment of Rs. 133 crores to a Turkish company, Karsan Private Limited, for the promised delivery of urea by February 1996, without any bank guarantee or insurance cover. The amount paid through the New York Branch of State Bank of India represented the total price of two lakh tons of Urea, but not a gram of urea was received in India in return. And the two key persons the Karsan company chief Tuncay Alankar and the vice-president Cihan Karanci who had come to India to finalise the deal in November

1995, became untraced when sought to be contacted. It was a copy book case of international swindle with active 'national' connivance and participation.

There was nothing right about the transaction from the word go. The provision for payment of the full amount in advance without any guarantee or cover was against all rules of ordinary business prudence. The post-haste payment of the amount to the Turkish firm by SBI working overtime flouted all guidelines relating to remittances abroad. Even the kickback of 4 million dollars was received by the Indian collaborators through dubious hawala channels smacking of FERA violation.

When the swindle came to light on non-receipt of urea in India by February 1996 as contracted, the CBI started investigation into the case. Sambasiva Rao, the Indian agent of the Turkish firm and kingpin of the scam, was arrested and interrogated by the CBI. He made a confessional statement according to which out of Rs. 133 crores paid by National Fertilizers Limited to the Turkish Company for nothing, Rs. 14 crores was the bribe money received by the Indian collaborators in this swindle. Sambasiva Rao confessed to have shared this amount with a relative of the then PM and son of the then Fertilizer Minister. The accused persons arrested and sent to Tihar jail included the relative of the PM, son of the Fertilizer Minister and Managing Director and Executive Director of National Fertilizers Limited.

The amount of money swindled in this case Rs.133 crores paid for nothing in return was not much. Nor was the bribe paid and received in the shady transaction Rs. 14 crores big enough to attract notice. It was the sheer audacity of the scamsters which shocked the people. It was as daring as broad day light robbery. For it happened in November 1995 when the air was thick with stories of corruption which had created a sensation and strong public opinion against it. The sugar import scandal was just about a year old and Jain Hawala scam was in advanced stage of investigation. Obviously the Indian collaborators of the Turkish swindlers felt cushioned against any action because of their political connection or perhaps the system had became so corrupt that no one looked around before indulging in corruption.

MPs Bribery Case

Even as corruption of Government functionaries for private profit was stalking the land, corruption of a different kind came to light. It could be summed up as corruption of the politicians by the politicians and for the politicians. Rumblings about bribing a few MPs of Jharkhand Mukti Morcha, a regional political party, by the ruling Congress party to win the vote of confidence in July 1993 had started doing the rounds in the wake of the unfolding of Jain Hawala Scam. In fact, there was a mention of S.K. Jain having paid hefty amount to some ruling party managers for effecting defections of some M.P.'s in his long confessional statement.

The matter came to a head on 28 February 1995 when one Rabindra Kumar, President Rashtria Mukti Morcha, filed a complaint before the CBI alleging that one Jharkhand Mukti Morcha MP had received Rs. 30 lakhs to vote against the no-confidence motion in July 1993. While the CBI was proceeding with the enquiry at a leisurely pace, the Delhi High Court intervened on being moved by the petitioner. On 24 May 1996, the High Court directed the CBI to register a regular case not only against the MP's who had received the bribe but also against the political leaders of the government who had negotiated and made the payments. The CBI understandably appealed to the Supreme Court against the High Court directive to register a case against its own masters. But the apex court upheld the High Court order. Accordingly, on 11 June 1996, the CBI registered a regular FIR against government leaders in the MP bribery case. The V.I.P's accused in the case included the ex-PM, Narsimha Rao, V.C. Shukla, R.K. Dhawan, Satish Sharma and others. It was a full blown case of political corruption which highlighted corruption not only of individuals but also of the system.

Sukhram Telecom Scam

In the midst of sensational corruption scandals sweeping the country, there was a bizarre case of petty corruption which could be viewed as a comic interlude. It involved a light weight ruling party leader of Himachal Pradesh-Sukhram. From a humble beginning, in the state politics, Sukhram had risen to be the

Communication Minister of the Government of India. The scam came to light when in August 1996, two cases were filed against the Minister after suit-cases stuffed with cash were seized from his houses in Delhi and Manali. The cash was the bribe money he received as quid pro quo for purchase of sub-standard telecom equipments as Union Communication Minister. In the context of the time-mid 1990's, when the stream of corruption was unplugged inundating the land. Sukhram's case was a relatively minor event like a drop in the stream. It was notable primarily for the manner in which a Minister took bribe in hard cash and deposited it in his house. No more than that.

The Bihar Animal Husbandry or Fodder Scam

Even by the standard of 1990's when corruption scandals were surfacing one after another without a break, the Bihar Animal Husbandry or Fodder Scam was a phenomenon which came to occupy the centre stage in corruption scenario. In regard to the scale, quantum and dimensions, it turned out to be a mega scam before which the other scams of the time paled into insignificance. And it was again a case of chance detection as in the case of Jain Hawala scam.

At a time when all concerned government functionaries had closed their eyes to the goings-on in the Animal Husbandry department for reasons to be explained a little later, a rather unconventional District Magistrate detected that the department in his district was drawing more money from the treasury than allotted or sanctioned for it. That sounded the alarm bell and led to a chain reaction of checkings and verifications in different district treasuries, state Finance Department and Accountant General's office. These belated efforts revealed a gaping hole through which hundreds of crores of public money had flown down to corrupt bureaucrats of the Animal Husbandry Department and their political Godfathers. As the illicit exercise continued unchecked, a whopping Rs. 950 crores was found to have been swindled by the scamsters over the years.

Facts speak more eloquently. In each of the years 1991-92. 1992-93 and 1993-94, the money withdrawn in excess of the grant was much more than the total grant itself. The figures:-

Year	Total Grant	Excess drawal
1991-92	Rs. 56,10,24144	Rs. 70,72,04886
1992-93	Rs. 66,93,35120	Rs. 87,77,27635
1993-94	Rs. 74,14,36274	Rs. 125,02,73056

And in the year 1995-96, an excess amount of about Rs. 80 crores over and above the sanction of Rs. 71-84 crores had already been drawn by the pampered department of Animal Husbandry in course of nine months only (up to December 1995). The repeated unchecked breaching of budget ceilings with the entire finance management looking the other way, allowed the scamsters to merrily go about their business of plunder.

When the scam erupted in February 1996, a bunch of criminal cases were registered at several police stations in the state in respect of fraudulent withdrawals and misappropriation of public money against an odd assortment of bureaucrats, treasury officials, fake suppliers etc. While minor police functionaries like Sub Inspectors of police stations concerned were going through the motion of routine investigation, petitions were filed in Patna High Court for ordering CBI investigation in view of the magnitude of the fraud. The State Government opposed the plea for investigation by CBI. That let the cat out of the bag casting suspicion on the conduct of the Government in this whole affair. For normally, the state governments all over the country opt for CBI investigation in such cases on their own to silence the critics and come clean, if they are clean. The fact that Bihar Government of that time opposed the plea for CBI investigation speaks for itself.

Rejecting the state government's pleas, the Patna High Court directed the CBI to take over the investigation of all cases registered at different police stations in connection with this scam and carry it to its "logical end". In its judgement dated 11 March 1996, the High Court concluded: "But from what has been seen above, it is clear that the excess drawals were not isolated acts, they were manifestations and result of well-knit conspiracy to commit loot and plunder of public money in a systematic manner, which could not be possible without the support of high-ups."

And further, in its long 43 page order, the High Court made some pungent observations and raised pertinent questions: "It is usual to find the treasury raising objections in passing bills-whether it is salary bill of the staff, fee bill of lawyers or contractor's bill. How then, without the financial sanction and availability of funds could money be drawn, to the tune of crores of rupees every year? Who permitted this excess expenditure?"

Inspite of such a clear and categorical verdict by the Patna High Court, the state government of the time tried its best to prevent CBI investigation into the scam. To forestall CBI stepping in to take up investigation, the state government filed an appeal in the Supreme Court against the order of the Patna High Court narrated above. That only showed how desperately the government of the day wanted to prevent thorough investigation into these cases of serial frauds by a specialist anti-corruption agency like the CBI. But the Supreme Court, being the apex court of justice, dismissed the state government's appeal and upheld the Patna High Court order directing the CBI to take up investigation. It was entirely due to the intervention of the High Court and Supreme Court that the CBI took up investigation of the Bihar Fodder scam cases and brought to light a major corruption story of the last decade of the 20th century. It was judicial activism at its best.

Before dwelling upon the result of CBI investigation, it would be interesting to have a glance at the modus operandi or modality of the swindle. Abhas Chatterji, a senior IAS officer of Bihar cadre, who took voluntary retirement during 1990's, wrote in an article in the *'The Times of India'*, Patna edition dated 21 February 1996: "It was one of those open secrets in the corridors of Patna Secretariat that everyone knew, talked and chuckled about, for the racket was known to enjoy powerful political patronage from the highest quarter....... It was only on paper we heard, that vet medicines were bought and distributed, on paper fodder and feed were purchased and consumed, on paper bulls were distributed and they all died and soon, we used to hear how 100 one-day old chicks became on paper 20 times in age and 50 times in number; how they had been duly vaccinated with Fl and F2 and yet had perished whole sale and soon". With crores upon crores of fake purchases of fodder, medicines and live-stock being made year after year without any check from any quarter, sky was the limit of public money gobbled up by the scamsters. The most shocking part of the scam was its daring openness and continuity beginning 1990-91 onwards with all controlling authorities keeping their eyes closed and mouth shut. How come?

There was a little background to the total dysfunction of the controlling or correcting mechanism allowing a free hand to the scamsters to carry on with their business of loot and plunder. Laloo Prasad who, by a quirk of destiny, became the Chief Minister of Bihar in 1990 riding on the wave of Mandal Commission movement, had an umbilical relation with the Animal Husbandry Department. He spent the best part of his student life in Patna, in course of which he became a prominent student leader, residing with his brother who was a Class IV employee of the Veterinary college. The Veterinary college campus, where his brother's quarter was located, was like his second home away from his village home in the interior of Bihar. So much so that when he ascended the throne of Bihar's Chief Ministership, he continued to live in that class four quarter of his brother in Veterinary college campus for quite some time before moving into the C.M.'s official residence. The government officials had a harrowing time providing the necessary facilities for him and his family in the cramped quarter of his brother in the veterinary college campus. While it sent a positive message of his plain and austere living, it also deepened his ties with the officials, contractors and suppliers of Animal Husbandry Department of which veterinary college was the main outlet.

This close relationship of the newly enthroned Chief Minister- Laloo Prasad - with officials of Animal Husbandry Department came in handy for them to encash and indulge in malpractices. The humble economic background of the new Chief Minister provided enough space for them to play for ingratiating themselves with him and enrich themselves in the process. For, inspite of his show of austere living to begin with, his large family had to be provided with creature's comforts befitting their new status as Bihar's first family. As such, Laloo Prasad's children had to be enrolled in costly boarding schools and other elite educational institutions. And he had a sizeable number of them to bring up and educate as he was the proud father of nine children. In fact, one of the principal scamsters was the local guardian of one or two of his sons admitted in a boarding school outside Patna. All this entailed high expenditure which posed no problem for Laloo Prasad, courtesy the officials and suppliers of the Animal Husbandry Department who were let free to compensate themselves for the services rendered.

It was in this background that the entire system of financial management and administrative propriety was struck with paralysis, leaving the scamsters free to carry on with plunder of public money under the implicit patronage of Laloo Prasad. The Chief Minister saw to it that his loyal flock of Animal Husbandry Department were adequately rewarded for the 'services' rendered. A notable example was the case of Shyam Bihari Sinha who had risen to become Regional Director of Animal Husbandry Department. As it turned out in course of CBI investigation, he was the kingpin or mastermind behind the scam and one of its principal beneficiaries. But significantly enough, he had been a favourite official of the department until the scam erupted. He was considered so indispensible by the Animal Husbandry Department that he was granted more than one extension of service after reaching the age of retirement. The last extension of service granted to him was a telling example of his political clout and privileged position he enjoyed with the government. He was to finally retire on 31.12.1993, but was given extension of one year upto 31.12.1994 in back date. The patent illegality of the process was highlighted in the Inspection Report of the Principal Accountant General, Bihar, on the fraudulent withdrawals during 1993-94 to 1995-96. The A.G. observed: "The Council of Ministers approved his extension on 13.06.1995, i.e., six months after the entire period of extension. It was noticed in this case that Sri Sinha was continued in his post after superannuation without the order of the competent authority, i.e., the Council of Ministers for the entire period of extension, which was illegal."

And he was not the only one to have become a hot favourite of the department for wrong reasons. There were other similarly favoured officials of the department who figured among the prominent accused in the scam cases. As the scandal started unfolding in all its ramifications, it appeared that the more favoured an official was in the department, the more deeply involved he was in the swindle. The irony of the situation could not be more evident.

At the end of the day, the sins of the swindlers caught up with them as the CBI was able to complete the investigation of the scam cases under the vigilant eye of the Patna High Court and Supreme Court. But not without hiccups due to pulls and pressures to derail the investigation on account of the clout Laloo Prasad enjoyed with the Central Government. And finally, the CBI filed chargesheets against Laloo Prasad and others in the concerned cases in June 1997. That brought to an end one of the most sensational corruption scandals of the closing years of the 20th century. For the Bihar Fodder Scam symbolized the total disruption or collapse of every mechanism that keeps a system functioning. There was no code that was not violated, no rule that was not by-passed, no financial or administrative norm that was not discarded to facilitate the swindle and open loot of public money by the corrupt brigade enjoying the blessings of the head of the government.

The tide of corruption scandals that swept the country during 1990's ebbed and waned towards the end of the 20th century. There was a noticeable lull in the surge of scams during the first few years of the 21st century. But as it turned out, it proved to be the proverbial lull before the storm. For the eruption of corruption scandals that shook the land from 2008 onwards dwarfed all the scams surfacing during 1990's as described above. The big scams that rocked the country after a short-lived interval are described below.

2G Spectrum Scam

In a nutshell, it related to under-charging mobile telephony companies for frequency allocation license in 2008. Stories of irregularities and corruption in frequency allocation to favourite companies by the Telecom Ministry of Government of India were circulating in political circles from the time it happened, but it did not come to public view for two years. It was the Comptroller and Auditor General (CAG) of India who took the lid off the mega scam which, according to the CAG's report, resulted in the loss of above one lakh crore of rupees to the government exchequer. In regard to its scale and dimensions, it is too big a scam to be summed up in this chapter. It has been dealt with at some length in Chapter 17.

Adarsh Housing Society Scam

It was a scam of a different kind involving top politicians and bureaucrats of Mahrashtra Government and military officers. The scam came to public view when the print and electronic media flashed it in a big way in 2010. The origins of the scam go back to the year 2002 when the Maharashtra Government was moved by the Adarsh Housing Society, a Mumbai based housing co-operative society, to allot land to build a residential complex for "the welfare of serving and retired personnel of defence services." According to media reports, the piece of land sought and obtained by the society, courtesy the Maharashtra Government, in the posh Colaba locality was reserved for war widows and army veterans of the Kargil War.

But in course of around ten years, the housing society constructed a building complex on the land in this prime locality and allotted flats to top politicians, their close relatives, bureaucrats and military officers at artificially lowered prices. In the process, the top brass of Maharashtra Government and the high profile beneficiaries of the scam bent several rules and indulged in various acts of omission and commission to get the flats allotted to themselves. The Comptroller and Accountant General of India (CAG) observed in his report in 2011: "The episode of Adarsh Co-operative Housing Society reveals how a group of select officials, placed in key posts, could subvert rules and regulations in order to grab prime government land a public property for personal benefit."

Some of the more glaring irregularities and blatant transgressions of rules included grant of No Objection Certificate from the Army to construction of the building in a sensitive coastal area, getting the MMRDA development plan modified and obtaining another No Objection for residential development in Coastal

Regulation Zone. The prized flats in the building were selectively allotted to politicians, bureaucrats and Army personnel who had nothing to do with the Kargil war. According to media reports, one ruling party politician was alleged to have grabbed a chunk of ten flats, which he had bought on behalf of top politicians.

When the scam erupted in a big way, many P.I.L. petitions were filed in Bombay High Court to monitor CBI investigation into the case which was started in January 2011. Pressed by the High Court to expedite the investigation, the CBI arrested several bigwigs in the case including two retired Major Generals, Adarsh Society promoter and others. And more importantly, the exposure of the scam led to the resignation of the then Chief Minister of Maharashtra Ashok Chavan. Two IAS officers of Maharashtra Government whose names figured in the scam were suspended.

The Maharashtra Government initiated course correction and damage control measures soon after the scam came to light. While on the one hand CBI was entrusted with investigation into the scams, the Govt. appointed a two member judicial commission under the Commissions of Enquiry Act to enquire into the alleged irregularities and corruption in the whole affair.

The Commonwealth Games Scam

The scam involved large scale misappropriation of money during the preparation and conduct of Commonwealth Games held in Delhi in 2010. It was a multi-faceted corruption scandal involving layers and layers of bribe money generated and distributed among diverse beneficiaries connected with organisation of the Games.

As usual, the scam was unearthed by the Comptroller and Accountant General. India's top watch dog over government's financial management, even before the games actually started. It may be noted that conduct of the Commonwealth Games was a costly affair involving huge expenditure to the tune of thousands of crores, much of it in the preparatory stage itself. Once the CAG opened the pandora's box, layers upon layers of corruption entailing loot of public money started unfolding. The media lapped it up in a big way leaving the public aghast and the Government wide-eyed. Everything from the constitution of the organising committee to the setting up of broadcast network of the Games was found to be tainted with corruption.

The Government responded by entrusting the CBI to investigate into the multiple corruption charges against the scamsters involving politicians, bureaucrats and corporates acting in collusion to manipulate and rob public money. The Prime Minister also set up a high level Shunglu Committee to enquire into the scam. Suresh Kalmadi, the Chairman of the Organising Committee and a sitting Congress M.P., and Lalit Bhanot, the Secretary General of the organising committee, were sacked from the committee in January 2011. Suresh Kalmadi was also arrested by the CBI in April 2011 after which he was suspended by the Congress Party. Others arrested by the CBI included T.S. Darbari, Joint Director General of the Organising Committee and Sanjay Mahindroo, Deputy Director General of the Organising Committee. It was alleged that various contracts connected with the games were manipulated by the organising committee and huge amounts misappropriated in the process.

Some of the notable allegedly corrupt transactions made by the organising committee's chairman and his team were as follows:

Illegitimate contracts were awarded to a Swiss firm for Timing-Scoring-Result system for the Games causing a loss of Rs. 95 crores to the exchequer.

The British authorities referred to the Indian High Commission a matter regarding hiring of London-based transport firm AM cars and vans at exorbitant prices and similar large payments to AM Films for installing video screens at the venue of the Queen's Baton Relay. The Enforcement Directorate registered a case under FEMA in this regard and took up investigation.

Another case was taken up by the CBI against officials of Mahanagar Telephone Nigam Limited and NOIDA based HCL Info systems for allegedly inflating the cost of setting up a broadcast network for the games by nearly Rs. 400 crores. It was alleged that MTNL awarded the work of broadcast network at an exorbitant price by manipulating specifications in such a manner as to make them tailor made for the private company HCL Infosystems. The CBI alleged that this change in specification, made in order to cause huge pecuniary benefit to HCL, led to the cost escalation from the initial estimate of about Rs. 31.43 crores to above Rs. 400 crores.

Infact, there was nothing right with the organising committee from the start. It was rumoured that late Sunil Dutt, the former Sports Minister, was opposed to Suresh Kalmadi heading the organising committee. There were several complaints regarding violation of norms in appointment of members of the committee resulting in nomination of some persons who had no expertise in the jobs meant for them. There were also complaints about the organising committee showing ghost employees on its muster roll.

Suresh Kalmadi, the principal accused in the Commonwealth Games Scam, was released on bail by Delhi High Court in January 2012. While CBI investigation and court proceedings kept moving at snail's speed, almost every accused in the scam was released on bail.

The visible and audacious corruption scandals, with wide ramifications, described in this Chapter formed the inglorious backdrop of the great anti-corruption movement launched by Anna Hazare in 2011. With such daring scams doing the rounds in the country, Anna's call for creation of a people's Ombudsman or Lok Pal had an instant appeal among the people when it was raised in a big way by Hazare in April and August 2011.

Even as the anti-corruption movement and Lok Pal debate were going on, another big scam relating to free allocation of millions of metric tons of coal blocks to private business entities by the Central Government without competitive bidding came to flight. As usual, it was brought out by CAG in his performance audit report submitted in 2012 on coal block allocations. The scam was too big to be dealt with in this chapter. For India's coal deposits are as valuable for the country as oil reserves are for Arab countries. And frittering away of this precious asset for private profit was not only appalling but sinful. This scam which came to be known as 'Coalgate' has been dwelt upon with all its wide implications in Chapter 22.

10

Critical Issues of the Lokpal Debate

There has been considerable debate over the merits and demerits of *The Lokpal Bill, 2011* introduced by the Government of India in August, 2011, *The Jan Lokpal Bill* of Anna's India Against Corruption (IAC) and *The Lokpal and Lokayuktas Bill, 2011* introduced by the Government in December, 2011. But these bills are not the only bills on Lokpal under circulation. Comprehensive suggestions have also been given by Aruna Roy's National Campaign for People's Right to Information (NCPRI) and Lok Satta of Jayaprakash Narayan, a former IAS officer and now an activist (not to be confused with the late JP).

The entire debate has brought forward certain critical issues for consideration, with divergent views and opinions having far reaching implications.

1. Composition and Appointment of Lokpal

The *Lokpal Bill, 2011* provides for a Chairperson who is or has been a Chief Justice of India or a Judge of the Supreme Court and up to eight members (with at least fifty per cent judicial members). The Jan Lokpal Bill provides for a Chairperson and ten members (with at least four members with legal background). The Chairperson should have extensive knowledge of law. According to *the Lokpal and Lokayuktas Bill*, 2011, the Lokpal shall consist of a Chairperson who is or has been a Chief Justice of the Supreme Court or an eminent person (with knowledge and expertise in anti-corruption policy, public administration, vigilance, finance, law and management) and such number of members, not exceeding eight, out of whom fifty per cent shall be judicial members. It also provides that not less than *fifty per cent* of the members of the Lokpal shall be from amongst the persons belonging to the *scheduled castes, schedules tribes, other backward classes, women and minorities*. Thus, for the first time, the concept of caste, religion and gender-based *reservation* is proposed to be introduced in the anti-corruption institutional framework.

According to the *Lokpal Bill, 2011*, the Chairperson and Members shall be appointed by the President on the recommendation of a Selection Committee which shall consist of the Prime Minister, Speaker, a Union Cabinet Minister (to be nominated by the PM). Leaders of the Opposition in both Houses, a Judge of Supreme Court, (to be nominated by the Chief Justice of India) a Chief Justice of a High Court (to be nominated by the Chief Justice of India) an eminent jurist, (to be nominated by the Central Govt.) an eminent person with knowledge of anti-corruption policy and public administration, vigilance, finance law or management (to be nominated by the Central Government). This Selection Committee may, if it considers necessary constitute a Search Committee of persons with expertise in anti-corruption policy, public administration, finance etc. for preparing a panel of names to be considered for appointment.

Under the **Jan Lokpal Bill,** the Chairperson and Members shall be appointed by the President on the recommendations of a *Selection Committee* which shall consist of the Prime Minister, Leader of the Opposition in the Lok Sabha, two judges of the Supreme Court, two Chief Justices of High Courts, (selected by a collegium of all Supreme Court Judges), the Chief Election Commissioner (CEC), the Comptroller and Auditor General (CAG), and all previous Chairpersons of the Lokpal.

- The Selection Committee shall select the Chairperson and the other members of the Lokpal from out of a short list prepared by a Search Committee.

- The *Search Committee* shall consist of 10 members. Five of its members shall be selected by the Selection Committee from amongst the retired Chief Justices of India, the retired Chief Election Commissioners and the retired Comptroller and Auditor Generals with impeccable reputation of integrity, who have not joined any political party after retirement and who are not holding any office under any government. The five members so selected shall, through consensus, co-opt another five members from the civil society in the search committee.

- The Search Committee before preparing the short list will invite nominations from such eminent individuals or such class of people, whom they deem fit, for the position of Chairperson or the members of the Lokpal.
- The recommendations about nominees should, interalia, contain details of any allegations faced by that candidate under any law, details of his work against corruption in the past, reasons why that person is suitable for the job and any other material that the search committee may decide.
- Such nominations as are received shall be put on a web site for inviting comments from the people with regard to the suitability or otherwise of the nominees.
- The Search Committee after taking into consideration the comments/information received from the public shall prepare, preferably through consensus, the short list of three times the number of persons to be appointed as members of the Lokpal.
- Any nominations to which objections are raised by any three members of the Search Committee shall not be included in the short list.
- Before sending the short list to the Selection Committee, the Search Committee will get the names of the short listed persons put on a public web site to enable people to send any relevant information/comments about the shortlisted persons.
- The Selection Committee shall, after considering all relevant

information about the short listed candidates, select the required number of persons preferably through consensus. However, a person shall not be selected if three members of the Selection Committee disapprove such name.

As per the **Lokpal and Lokayuktas Bill, 2011,** the Chairperson and Members shall be appointed by the President on the recommendations of a Selection Committee consisting of the Prime Minister, the Speaker, the Leader of the Opposition in the Lok Sabha, the Chief Justice of India (or a Judge of the Supreme Court nominated by him) and one eminent jurist nominated by the President. The Selection Committee shall constitute a Search Committee of at least seven members for preparing a panel of names to be considered, provided that not less than fifty per cent of the members of the Search Committee shall be from amongst persons belonging to SC/ST, OBC, women and minorities. Hence, the principle of reservation has been reiterated in the bill.

2. Inclusion of Prime Minister under Jurisdiction of Lokpal

The **Lokpal Bill, 2011** excludes the Prime Minister from the jurisdiction of Lokpal in investigations against corruption. The PM can be covered only after he has demitted office. On the other hand, the **Jan Lokpal Bill** includes the PM without exceptions. The **NCPRI Bill** takes a middle path and includes the PM with certain safeguards: (a) the full bench of the Lokpal shall refer the complaint to the Chief Justice of India who shall refer it to the full bench of the Supreme Court. (b) It excludes the PM in cases where he is not directly *involved* (C) *If the PM felt that any information would compromise national security; CJI* would decide after a briefing by PM whether the information should be disclosed.

The **Lokpal and Lokayuktas Bill, 2011** includes the Prime Minister in the jurisdiction, with the exception of matters relating to *international relations, external and internal security, public order, atomic energy and space.* It also stipulates that no inquiry shall be conducted unless a full bench of the Lokpal considers the initiation of inquiry and at least three-forth of its members approves of such inquiry.

In this connection, it is interesting to note that *Article 361* of **The Constitution of India** provides legal protection to the President of India and Governors of States as under: 361 (2) : *"No criminal proceedings whatsoever shall be instituted or continued against the President, or the Governor of a State, in any court during his term of office".*

(3) : *"No process for the arrest or imprisonment of the President, or the Governor of a State, shall issue from any court during his term of office".*

No such legal protection is provided to the Prime Minister under the Indian Constitution.

3. Parliamentary Privileges

Parliamentary privilege is a legal immunity enjoyed by members of certain legislatures, in which legislators are granted protection against civil or criminal liability for actions done or statements made related to one's duties as a legislator. It is common in countries whose constitutions are based on the Westminster system. In the United Kingdom, it allows members of the House of Lords and House of Commons to speak freely during ordinary parliamentary proceedings without fear of legal action on the grounds of slander, contempt of court or breaching the Official Secrets Act. *The ancient and undoubted rights and privileges of the Commons* are claimed by the Speaker at the beginning of each new Parliament. The House itself is the only judge of its own privileges. In this regard, India continues to be broadly governed by British Parliamentary Conventions.

Article 105 of the **Constitution of India** provides for privileges and immunities of the members of the Houses of the Parliament. Accordingly of Article 105 (2):

"No member of Parliament shall be liable of any proceedings in any court in respect of anything said or any note given by him in Parliament or any Committee thereof, and no person shall be so liable in respect of the publication by or under the authority of either House of Parliament of any report, paper, notes or proceedings."

The **Lokpal Bill, 2011** recognizes this constitutional position and stipulates that the Lokpal shall not inquire into any matter involved in, or arising from, or connected with, any such allegation of corruption against any Member of either House of Parliament in respect of anything said or a vote given by him in Parliament or any committee thereof covered under the provisions contained in clause (2) of Article 105 of the Constitution. The same is reiterated in the **Lokpal and Lokayuktas Bill, 2011.** This constitutional protection is proposed to be removed under the **Jan Lokpal Bill.**

4. Judicial Independence

The proposed inclusion of judiciary under the jurisdiction of Lokpal under the **Jan Lokpal bill** has raised serious issues about the need for independence of judiciary and separation of powers. The NCPRI is also of this view arguing that the independence of the judiciary should not be undermined. The solution apparently lies in a separate law to deal with judicial corruption instead of vesting an all-powerful Lokpal with the jurisdiction to conduct inquiry against the judges. The Government of India has introduced the **Judicial Standards and Accountability Bill, 2010** that tries to lay down enforceable standards of conduct for judges. The bill requires, inter alia, the judges to declare assets owned by them and their family members and seeks to create mechanisms for lodging of complaints against judges. The bill remains pending in Parliament.

5. Federal Issues and Center-state Relations

It has been pointed that the Central Government mandating for Lokayuktas in the States can compromise the *"federal"* principles of the Constitution and impinge upon the constitutional jurisdiction of the States. The Center can at best pass an enabling law under Article 252 of the Constitution (Power of parliament to legislate for two or more states by consent and adoption of such legislation by any other state), or a *model* law, but *not* a *binding law.*

On the contrary, it has been argued that India is a signatory of the **UN Convention Against Corruption (UNCAC), 2003** which, inter alia, provides for setting up of anti-corruption bodies with "necessary independence" to carry out their functions effectively" (Art 6 (2), UNCAC). Further, Article 253 of the **Constitution of India** authorizes the Parliament to legislate for giving effect to international agreements as under:

"Notwithstanding anything in the foregoing provisions of this Chapter, Parliament has power to make law for the whole or any part of the territory of India for implementing any treaty, agreement or convention with any other country or countries or any decision made at any international conference, association or other body".

Thus, according to this view, under the above provision, the Parliament has the power to make laws for the entire territory of India even on *"state" subjects.*

The **Lokpal Bill, 2011** provides for only a Lokpal at the centre. The **Jan Lokpal Bill** states that provisions similar to Lokpal should be made for State level Lokayuktas and incorporated in the Bill. As the name suggests, the **Lokpal and Lokayuktas Bill, 2011** has incorporated provisions on Lokayuktas in the States in extensive detail covering Part III of the Bill from Sections 63 to 97.

It may be recalled that on August 27, 2011, both the Houses of Parliament passed ***"Sense of the House"*** **Resolutions** agreeing, in principle, on the following key issues: *Citizens' Charter, Lower Bureaucracy* also to be under the Lokpal through "appropriate mechanism", and establishment of *Lokayuktas in the States.* And on Sunday, 28 August, 2011, the 13th morning of his fast, Anna broke his high-profile fast by sipping coconut water. But when the bill on Lokayuktas was introduced in the Parliament in December 2011, it was opposed by almost all the opposition parties and Trinamool Congress, an ally of the UPA Government on grounds of "federalism" and this became one of the major reasons for the failure of the bill in the Rajya Sabha. Ironically, this was one of the few issues on which the Government appeared to be on the same page with Team Anna.

6. Autonomy of The Investigating Agency

According to the **Lokpal Bill, 2011,** the Lokpal shall

constitute an Investigation Wing for the purpose of conducting investigation of an alleged offence. Under the **Jan Lokpal Bill,** the anti-corruption branch of the CB1 will come under the Lokpal. The Central Government will cease to have any control over personnel belonging to this branch. The *Delhi Special Police Establishment Act, 1946* (from which the CBI derives authority), would stand amended accordingly. The **Lokpal and Lokayuktas Bill, 2011** provides for an Inquiry Wing and a Prosecution Wing of the Lokpal and similar structures for the Lokayuktas. The Lokpal can get preliminary inquiry against a public servant conducted by its inquiry wing or any agency (including Delhi Special Police Establishment, i.e., CBI). The complaints shall be referred to the Central Vigilance Commission (CVC), which shall send its report on the matter, in respect of Group A and Group B officers, back to Lokpal for further decision and, with respect to Group C and Group D employees, the Commission shall take action in exercise of its own powers under the **Central Vigilance Commission Act, 2003,** subject to reporting and review mechanism by the Lokpal. On the crucial question of autonomy of the investigating agency, the Bill states that the Lokpal shall have the powers of *"superintendence and direction"* over the CBI in respect of the matters referred to CBI by the Lokpal for preliminary inquiry or investigation provided that, while exercising powers of superintendence or giving directions, the Lokpal shall not exercise powers in such a manner so as to require the agency to investigate a case in a particular manner.

In other words, under this Bill, the CBI remains under the Government, subject to superintendence of the Lokpal in cases referred to it for inquiry. This has led to criticism over the reluctance of the government of the day to cease control over this premiere investigating agency of the country which, it is alleged, has been misused by successive governments from time to time to settle political scores. However, the Bill does provide that the Director of the CBI shall be appointed by the Government on the recommendation of a Committee consisting of the Prime Minister, the Leader of the Opposition in the Lok Sabha and the Chief Justice of India (or a Judge of the Supreme Court nominated by the Chief Justice).

The role of the CBI as an investigating agency and the institutional loop holes has been discussed in detail in another chapter of this book.

7. Legal Protection to Public Servants

Under Section 19 of **Prevention of Corruption Act (PCA), 1988,** no Court shall take cognizance of an offence punishable under the Act alleged to have been committed by a public servant, except with the *previous sanction* :-

(a) In the case of a person who is employed in connection with the affairs of the Union and is not removable from his office save by or with the sanction of the Central Government, of that Govt.

(b) In the case of a person who is employed in connection with the affairs of a State and is not removable from his office save by or with the sanction of the State Govt. of that Govt.

(c) In the case of any other person, of the authority competent to remove him from his office.

According to Section 197 of **Code of Criminal Procedure (Cr PC), 1973:**

(1) When any person who is or was a judge or magistrate or a public servant not removable from his office save by or with the sanction of the Government is accused of any offence alleged to have been committed by him while acting or purporting to act *in the discharge of his official duty,* no Court shall take cognizance of such offence except with the previous sanction:

(a) In the case of a person who, at the time of commission of the alleged offence, was employed in connection with the affairs of the Union, of the Central Government.

(b) In the case of a person who was employed in connection with the affairs of a State, of the State Government.

(2) No court shall take cognizance of any offence alleged to

have been committed by any member of the Armed Forces of the Union while acting or purporting to act in the discharge of his official duty, except with the previous sanction of the Central Government.

The above provisions in PCA and CrPC stand amended under the **Lokpal Bill, 2011** as no previous sanction from the Government would be required in corruption cases. Similarly, under the Jan **Lokpal Bill,** any permission which is required under any law for initiating investigation or prosecution under any Act shall be deemed to have been granted once the Lokpal has granted permission to initiate investigation or prosecution for any offences under Prevention of Corruption Act. The same position has been reiterated in the **Lokpal** and **Lokayuktas Bill, 2011** under Section 23 that makes it clear that previous sanction will not be necessary for investigating and initiating prosecution by the Lokpal in such cases. This is a significant step forward in anti-corruption procedure on which unanimity appears to have been achieved but rarely highlighted in the public debate on the entire issue.

8. Inclusion of NGOs and Corporates

The **Lokpal Bill, 2011** seeks to bring within the ambit of Lokpal corruption related activities of any "society or association of persons or trust in receipt of any donation from the public and the annual income of which exceeds such amount as the Central Government may by notification specify." The **Jan Lokpal Bill,** in contrast, does not specify NGOs. It is alleged that this apparent partiality towards NGOs is due to the NGO background of several prominent members of team Anna. However, the Jan Lokpal bill does mention about corporate corruption and empowers the Lokpal to recommend cancellation or modification of a lease, license, permission, contract or agreement if it was obtained by corrupt means and to recommend blacklisting of a firm, company or any other person involved in an act of corruption by the public authority.

The **Lokpal and Lokayuktas Bill, 2011** also seeks to bring within the ambit of Lokpal corruption related activities of any society or association of persons or trust in receipt of any donation from the public and the annual income of which exceeds such amount as the Central Government may by notification specify or from any foreign source under the **Foreign Contribution Regulation Act, 2010** in excess of ten lakh rupees in a year or such higher amount as the Government may, by notification, specify.

9. Action on False and Frivolous Complaints

The **Lokpal Bill, 2011** provides that whoever makes any false and frivolous or vexatious compliant under the Act shall, on conviction, be punished with imprisonment for a term which shall not be less than two years but which may extend to five years and with fine which shall not be less than Rs. 25,000 but which may extend to two lakh rupees. This *provision has* been criticized *as* being *too* harsh *and* can *even* act *as a* deterrent against lodging of complaints in genuine cases also. The **Jan Lokpal Bill** prescribes only fine not exceeding Rs. One lakh in such cases. Under the **Lokpal** and **Lokayuktas Bill, 2011,** the prescribed punishment is imprisonment for a term which may extend to one year and with fine which may extend to one lakh rupees.

10. Interception of Communication and Privacy Rights

The **Jan Lokpal Bill** empowers the Lokpal to approve interception and monitoring of messages or data or voice transmitted through telephones, internet or any other medium as per rules under **Indian Telegraph Act** read with Information Technology Act. This provision has raised concerns about privacy rights and freedom of expression. Under the Telegraph Act, this is permitted only on grounds of sovereignty and integrity of India, security, public order and prevention of incitement of an offence. The Supreme Court in 1997 had laid down certain procedural safeguards. Giving this power to the lokpal raises debates about the possibility of lokpal becoming "too" powerful that could be detrimental to civil liberties and right to privacy.

11. Centralisation of Powers

Aruna Roy's **NCPRI** has proposed a ***"basket of measures"*** in place of an ***omnibus law*** that vests all powers and responsibilities in a single institution of Lokpal. The NCPRI position is that over-loading one institution would make for an impossible agenda and giving widespread powers to an unelected body could be a threat to democracy. The NCPRI proposed three different institutions:

(a) A national anti-corruption commission called **Lokpal**, to tackle corruption of all elected representatives and senior bureaucrats.

(b) Strengthening of **Central Vigilance Commission (CVC)** to be an investigative and prosecution authority for the remaining category of public servants.

(c) A judicial accountability commission to investigate charges of corruption against judges.

(d) Strengthening the Whistle Blower Protection Bill under process with the Parliament.

"Regarding Citizens" Charter, the NCPRI holds that the Lokpal should not be involved in grievance redressal because it is impractical. It proposes a separate national grievance redressal bill to cover the complaints that arise in the delivery of services in a decentralized and time bound manner. On the other hand, team Anna insists that grievance redressal should come under Lokpal because "repeated violation of citizen charter by any public servant" has been defined as one of the "acts of corruption" under **Jan Lokpal bill.**

The Lok Satta model of Jai Prakash Narayan is somewhat similar to that of NCPRI. According to Lok Satta, the CVC (Chairman and two members) should be ex-officio members of the Lokpal and be appointed in the same manner. Allegations against Group "A" officers will be dealt with by the lokpal and lower categories of public servants will be dealt by the CVC. Once the CVC is integrated with the Lokpal, that body will exercise superintendence and guidance of the CBI. The CBI should be divided into two agencies -crime investigation wing and anti-corruption wing. The anti-corruption wing of CBI would be accountable only to the CVC. In states, the anti-corruption bureau would be directly under the Lokaykta. The Lok Satta agrees with the NCPRI that grievance redressal should not be part of the lokpal's jurisdiction but should come under grievance redressal authorities to the formed at the Center and the States.

Both Anna's IAC and Aruna Roy's NCPRI, however, agree that the Lokpal, as an institution should be replicated at the State level through appropriate Lokayuktas. The Lok Satta also agrees with the same.

12. Whistle Blower Protection

A ***whistle blower*** is a person who tells the public or someone in authority about alleged dishonest or illegal activities occurring in a public or private organiration. Most of the whistle blowers are internal, but they can also be external. No provision for the same has been made in the **Lokpal Bill, 2011.** On the other hand, the **Jan Lokpal Bill** provides for protection of whistle blowers in specific terms as under:

- It shall be the duty of the Lokpal to provide full protection to whistle blowers from any physical harm or administrative harassment. Identity of such whistle blowers shall also be protected if the whistle blower so desires. For achieving this objective it shall be competent for the Lokpal to give suitable direction to security agencies for providing security as well as to any other authority to ensure that no harassment is caused to such whistle blower.

- Orders under this section shall be passed expeditiously and in any case within a month of receipt of complaint. Immediate action will be taken in cases involving a threat of physical victimisation.

- The investigations in complaints by whistle blowers facing physical or professional victimisation shall be fast tracked and completed within three months of receipt of the same.

The **Lokpal and Lokayuktas Bill, 2011** does not contain any provision for whistle blower protection. However, the Government of India has introduced the **Public Interest**

Disclosure and Protection of Persons Making the Disclosure Bill, 2010. Commonly known as the Whistle blowers' Bill, it seeks to protect whistle blowers, i.e., persons making a public interest disclosure related to an act of corruption, misuse of power or criminal offence by a public servant. It designates the Central and State Vigilance Commissions to receive disclosures and lays down safeguards for protection of whistleblowers. The Bill was referred to the Standing Committee on Personnel, Public Grievances, Law and Justice. The Committee presented its report in June 2011. The Bill, that seeks to address the issue outside the lokpal framework, remains pending in Parliament.

13. Citizens Charter

The **Lokpal Bill, 2011** and the **Lokpal and Lokayuktas Bill, 2011** do not have provisions for a Citizen Charter for grievance redressal. On the other hand, the **Jan Lokpal Bill** provides for elaborate provisions in this regard as under:

- Each public authority shall prepare a specific charter within a reasonable time not exceeding one year from the coming into force of this Act.
- Every citizens' charter shall enumerate the public authority's commitments to the citizens which are capable of being met within a specific time limit and shall designate the officer whose duty would be to fulfill the commitment of the public authority.
- If any public authority does not prepare its citizen's charter within a year, Lokpal shall notify the citizen's charter on its own after consulting the public authority and the same shall be binding on that authority.
- Each public authority shall designate an official called *Public Grievance Redressal Officer* in each station where the public authority has an office, to whom a complaint could be made for any violation of the citizens' charter.
- It shall be the duty of the Grievance Redressal Officer

to get the grievance redressed within a period of 30 days from the receipt of the complaint.

- In the event of even the Grievance Redressal Officer not getting the grievance redressed within the specific period of 30 days a complaint could be made to the Lokpal.

- The Lokpal after hearing the Grievance Redressal Officer would impose suitable penalty not exceeding Rs. 500/- for each day's delay but not exceeding Rs. 50,000/- to be recovered from the salaries of the Grievance Redressal Officer.

- Apart from levying the penalty on the Grievance Redressal Officer, the Lokpal may also in suitable cases recommend to the appropriate authority to have departmental punishment imposed on the Grievance Redressal Officer.

- There shall be at least one officer of the Lokpal in each district to receive grievances who shall be called an ***Appellate Grievance Officer.*** However, in such places where there is more concentration of central government offices, there shall be more Appellate Grievance Officers as may be required.

- A social audit of each Appellate Grievance Officer shall take place every six months, in which he shall present himself before the public, present the data related to his functioning, respond to public queries and incorporate suggestions from public in his functioning. The public hearing shall be attended by a senior officer from Lokpal.

The Government of India has introduced in December, 2011 a separate bill on the subject known as **The Right of Citizens for Time Bound Delivery of Goods and Services and Redressal of their Grievance Bill, 2011.** The Bill, inter alia, makes it mandatory for every public authority to publish a Citizen's Charter within six months that shall include:

(a) details of the goods and services provided by a public authority,

(b) name of the person or agency responsible for providing the goods and services,

(c) time frame within which such goods and services have to be provided,

(d) category of people entitled to the goods and services,

(e) details of the complaints redressal mechanism.

With many bills connected with Lokpal issue doing the rounds, Anna's Jan Lokpal Bill stands intact in one piece. The Bill provides for appointment of Grievance Redressal Officers, State Public Grievance Redressal Commission and Central Public Redressal Commission with designated appellate authorities.

14. Lokpal as a Constitutional Body

During the "historic" parliamentary debate on 27th August' 2011, Rahul Gandhi put forward the proposal to confer "constitutional" status to the Lokpal. Touted as a "game changer", it seeks to elevate the status of the Lokpal. Critics of the suggestion alleged that this may delay the process as a constitutional amendment would require two-thirds majority in both Houses of Parliament- a difficult proposition in an era of coalition politics. The Government of India introduced the **Constitutional (116th Amendment) Bill, 2011** in December to confer constitutional status to the Lokpal and Lokayuktas but the Bill could not be passed. A closer look shows that the issues involved are far more complicated. As discussed earlier, several provisions of the Jan Lokpal Bill have constitutional implications. What matters is the substance and efficacy of anti-corruption institution to deal with the menace of corruption, rather than status and semantics.

11

Loopholes in the Anti-corruption Regime

It has now to be examined how the institution of Lokpal would be an improvement over the existing anti-corruption regime in the country. In other words, what is the need for setting up a new and unknown anti-corruption institution in the first place, when institutions like CVC, C.B.I and State Vigilance Bureaus are already in place? The rough and ready answer to that would be the all too evident mounting incidence of corruption in the country, as touched upon in earlier chapters, inspite of the existing anti-corruption institutions in operation. In normal course, that should be evidence enough to stop any further debate on the issue of need for a Lokpal in India. It is proved by the fact that the need was felt as early as 1968 when the first Lokpal Bill was moved. Since then successive governments at the Centre have been bringing up Lokpal Bills from time to time, though failing to actually enact them.

The need for a new anti-corruption regime under Lokpal arises out of the failure of the existing institutional and legal frame work in stemming the root of corruption. First, the legal aspect. The entire anti-corruption exercise under the existing arrangement is based on two foundational laws - the Indian Penal Code (IPC) and Prevention of Corruption Act (PCA). The Indian Penal Code enacted by the British rulers in 1860 for the first time defined bribery and corruption on the part of government employees as crime and provided for punishment for that vide Sections 161 to 165. The important fact is that bribery and corruption are put in the same category as any other crime like murder, dacoity, theft etc. And yet the Code of Criminal Procedure (Cr. P. C.) enacted by the colonial regime prescribed a rider of *previous sanction* for prosecuting the corrupt government employees. This placed a government employee in a class apart and above the common citizen in respect of crime, as defined in the Penal Code, and prosecution for it. That is, no government employee could be prosecuted for any offence committed in discharge of his official duty without previous sanction of the government concerned. This has since been incorporated in the fresh code of Criminal Procedure (Cr. P. C) adopted in 1973 vide Section 197.

Since the British rulers were totally dependent on government employees to carry on with their rule, this rider of previous sanction was introduced to keep up the loyalty by providing them with this cushion against prosecution. By incorporating it in the amended Cr. P. C. of 1973, the outdated legacy of the British rule was carried forward.

The rider of "previous sanction" has been more specifically prescribed in the Prevention of Corruption Act which is the bedrock of entire anti-corruption effort of the Government. It may be noted that, as mentioned earlier, the Prevention of Corruption Act was also the gift of the colonial regime which enacted it in February 1947, just before the advent of India's Independence. This Act of February 1947 more emphatically provided that no court could take cognizance. of an offence punishable under it without the "previous sanction" of the competent authority. This restrictive proviso has been fully replicated and elaborated in the amended Prevention of Corruption Act of 1988 vide Section 19. In case of central government employees, previous sanction of central government and in case of state government employees, that of the state government concerned, is necessary for prosecution in cases of corruption.

As explained above, the whole idea behind this restrictive proviso of "previous sanction" was to create a favoured class of bureaucrats, who were the pillars of the colonial regime. This unholy legacy of the colonial regime was faithfully carried forward by the bureaucrats of independent India and their political bosses for obvious reasons. They relished being in the privileged class apart from and above the common citizen in respect of the operation of anti-corruption laws.

According to Section 19 of the Prevention of Corruption Act. no court can take cognizance of a corruption case against any "public servant" without previous sanction of the competent authority. This provision for mandatory sanction of the competent authority before prosecuting any "public servant" for corrupt practice has robbed it of much of its effectiveness in combating corruption. In terms of the existing legal position, only the authority competent to remove a public servant from office is competent to sanction prosecution against him. While the authority so competent to sanction prosecution against a government or semi-government employee is identifiable, it is not so easy in case of Ministers and legislators who, according to settled law, are also clubbed as "public servants".

Technically, the Governor of a State is the competent authority to sanction the prosecution of Ministers and Chief Minister of the State, because he is the *de jure* authority to remove them from office. But according to Article 163 of the Constitution, the Governor is only the constitutional Head of the State government and has to act only on the advice of the Council of Ministers. In all matters of state administration, the *de-facto* executive authority lies with the Council of Ministers. Accordingly, strictly speaking, the Council of Ministers itself has the power to sanction the prosecution of a Minister or Chief Minister. This problem has, however, been put under the carpet by the settled practice of the Governor of a State sanctioning prosecution of the Chief Minister.

But what about the legislators-M.P.'s, M.L.A.'s and M.L.C.'s? They are elected by the people for a fixed term and can be removed only by the electorate at the end of their term. Who then would be the competent authority to sanction the prosecution of an M.L.A or M.P under the Prevention of Corruption Act?

This was a moot point which had to be settled by judicial verdict affirming that the Presiding Officer of the House to which the legislator was elected would be the competent authority to sanction his prosecution in cases of corruption.

Though rare, but in recent times, charges of corruption on the part of some members of higher judiciary have come to light. Their tenure is secured and they can be removed only through impeachment by both Houses of Parliament. If, as a public servant, a member of higher judiciary is to be prosecuted under the Prevention of Corruption Act, sanction would have to be obtained from both Houses of Parliament.

That would go to show how cumbersome the whole process of prosecution for corruption has become on account of the mandatory provision for sanction by the competent authority. It has blunted the cutting edge of the anti-corruption regime and made it largely ineffective in checking corrupt practices by public servants. This is reflected in large number of cases of corruption remaining pending with different government departments at the State and Central level for grant of sanction for long periods. Meanwhile, the public servants concerned remain free to carry on with their corrupt practices. Some of them even get plum postings and continue to flourish even as corruption cases against them remain pending for sanction indefinitely. This is nothing but travesty of the anti-corruption regime that is in place. In simple terms what is provided by the anti-corruption law to curb corruption is taken away by the mandatory sanction proviso under Section 19 of the Prevention of Corruption Act of 1988.

Looking at it from any angle, mandatory sanction in corruption cases not only puts a brake on the progress of such cases but is entirely redundant and unwarranted. A corruption charge against a public functionary is first thoroughly investigated by a professional investigating agency- the CBI or the State Vigilance Bureau or the State Police-in accordance with law. And on submission of charge sheet, it is thrashed out by a court of law where the charged functionary has full opportunity to counter the charge and defend himself. Where is the space for a third intermediary agency to sit in judgement over the charge before the judiciary takes over which alone has the legitimacy to judge? It amounts to an undue interference in the course of justice established by law. It cannot be justified on any count.

That brings up the pertinent question-why was it placed in the anti-corruption law at all? The answer is simple. As mentioned earlier, it was the legacy of the colonial regime which first incorporated it in the original Prevention of Corruption Act of February 1947. For the Indian bureaucracy was the pillar of the British rule in India. The colonial regime had created a privileged class of so-called public servants apart from and above the common citizens. It was to protect this privileged class from too much exposure to common citizens' scrutiny of their work and conduct that the colonial rulers introduced this proviso of mandatory sanction even as they brought up the Anti-Corruption Act to tackle growing incidence of corruption. It was kind of a parting gift by them to the Indian bureaucracy. And it was gratefully accepted by independent India's ruling class to preserve their privileged status in regard to allegations of corruption.

This loophole in the existing anti-corruption regime is sought to be plugged in the proposed Lokpal regime. The Jan Lokpal Bill of Anna's team brushes aside the question of any permission or sanction for investigation or prosecution in cases of corruption altogether. Once the Lokpal has granted permission to initiate investigation or prosecution for any offence under the Prevention of Corruption Act, that would be deemed to be permission requested under any Act or law. And the Government Lokpal Bill also proposes to omit the provision for sanction in investigation of corruption cases. It specifically provides that no sanction would be required by the Lokpal under 197 of Cr. P.C. and Section 19 of the Prevention of Corruption Act to deal with any complaint against a public servant. To that extent, the Lokpal regime would be a definite improvement over the existing anti-corruption regime in combating corruption.

That partly answers the question posed at the beginning of this chapter-why have the Lokpal at all? That is, in regard to the big legal loophole that Lokpal would plug and which has proved to be a big hurdle in dealing with the corrupt, the need for Lokpal becomes all too evident. But there is another gaping institutional loophole in the existing system which further re-enforces the need for the new institution of Lokpal. This is being dealt with in the next chapter.

12

The Institutional Loophole

The most important institution of the existing anti-corruption regime is the C.B.I. It is the sole instrument or the working arm of the government of India to deal with corruption. It is a well organised body equipped with selected police and legal professionals to carry on with the task of catching the corrupt and prosecuting them in courts of law.

To begin from the beginning, it may be noted that what has now come to be known as CBI (Central Bureau of Investigation) was originally the Delhi Special Police establishment created to deal with the growing incidence of corruption among central government employees in the wake of the second world war. It was conceived as out and out a police unit designed to enquire and investigate into cases of corruption among central government employees as a specialist organisation. It was brought into being by the Delhi Special Police Establishment Act 1946, a year before India's independence.

Incidentally, the second world war was kind of a catalyst for installation of watchdog bodies all over the world. It was in the period after the second world war that the institutions of ombudsman were established in around a hundred countries in varying forms depending upon their varying situations and requirements. More about the institution of ombudsman in another chapter.

To continue with the story of the Delhi Police Establishment, it remained a rather low profile institution in the immediate post-independence years for the simple reason that the incidence of corruption during that period was rather negligible. When symptoms of corruption on the part of government functionaries started surfacing, a committee on prevention of corruption was set up for the first time in independent India under the Chairmanship of K. Santhanam in 1962 to address the problem. The committee submitted its report in March 1964. It was as a follow up action that the Central Bureau of Investigation (CBI) was created as a specialist central police unit to investigate into charges of corruption against 'public servants' and prosecute them in courts of law. Its legal status, powers and jurisdiction were defined by the Delhi Special Police Establishment Act of 1946. Thus Delhi Special Police Establishment, created by the colonial regime to tackle corruption among small time 'public servants', emerged in its new avatar of C.B.I. to curb corruption, which was fast spreading among government employees, in a more systematic way.

It is, however, ironic that just when C.B.I. was set up to tackle corruption of government functionaries in a more organised way, its freedom to act against members of higher bureaucracy involved in corruption was sought to be curtailed. The overall administrative control of the Delhi Special Police Establishment i.e. the CBI vests in the central government under section 4(1) of the Delhi Special Police Establishment Act, which governs the C.B.I. It functions under the general 'Superintendence' of the central government. There can be no problem with that as long as 'Superintendence' did not interfere with actual investigation of an offence by CBI in accordance with law. But the central government, under its power of 'superintendence', issued the single directive No. 4.7(3) restricting the powers of the CBI to initiate investigation against civil servants who are 'decision making officers'. This single Directive protected the higher bureaucracy who were described as 'decision making officers' in a veiled way.

This executive order provided that the CBI could not initiate any preliminary enquiry and institute any regular case into charges of corruption against 'public servants' of the rank of Joint Secretary to central government and above *without prior permission of the Central government*. This executive directive was even more draconian than the provision under section 19 of the Prevention of Corruption Act requiring prior sanction of competent authority for prosecution of the corrupt. The restriction under the Prevention of Corruption Act operated only *at the stage of taking cognizance of the offence in court.* But the above single Directive *prevented the CBI even from starting any investigation without the permission of the government* where public servants of the rank of Joint Secretary and above are involved.

This crippling executive directive made the CBI, the working arm of the existing anticorruption regime, almost powerless against corruption on the part of higher bureaucracy and those above them, that is, the Ministers. The directive of the central government under its power of, general 'Superintendence' over CBI was palpably wrong and untenable. For law does not classify offenders according to their status in life. Every person accused of committing an offence is to be dealt within the same manner, irrespective of their official or social status, in accordance with law.

Accordingly, this government directive for taking prior permission before registering preliminary enquiry or regular case was challenged in the Supreme Court. In the concerned case, Vineet Narain V/s the Union of India (1998), the Supreme Court passed a clear order declaring that any such executive instruction to CBI (requiring prior permission for investigation) was illegal. The court observed: "once the jurisdiction is conferred on the CBI to investigate an offence by virtue of notification under section 3 of the Act (Delhi Special Police Establishment Act, 1946), the powers of investigation are governed by the statutory provisions and they cannot be stopped or curtailed by any executive instruction issued under section 4(1) thereof....................It is settled that statutory jurisdiction cannot be subject to executive control. And further, "In absence of any statutory requirement of prior permission or sanction for investigation, it cannot be imposed as a condition precedent for initiation of the investigation once jurisdiction is conferred on the CBI to investigate the offence by virtue of the notification under section 3 of the Act."

The judicial verdict of the highest court of the country was a clear enough guide to allow the CBI a freehand in initiating preliminary enquiry and regular case into complaints of corruption against higher bureaucracy and Ministers. But instead of accepting the categorical verdict of the Supreme Court in good grace, the government proceeded to find a way to circumvent it. It may be noted that the Supreme Court had struck down the executive order requiring prior permission on the ground that it was not a statutory requirement under the Delhi Special Police Establishment Act 1946 which governed the CBI. The government, therefore, decided to re-introduce the single directive requiring prior permission by incorporating it in Section 3 of the Act itself to make it a statutory requirement. And to accomplish it the matter was placed in the concerned Standing committee of parliament which recommended that the Act be amended to give statutory status to the above executive directive. Accordingly the Delhi Special Police Establishment Act, 1946 was amended to provide for prior permission of government for initiating preliminary enquiry and regular case into corruption charges against higher bureaucracy and Ministers. Thus what was not provided for in the original Delhi Special Police Establishment Act 1946 even by the colonial regime to shield senior functionaries of the government against preliminary enquiry and regular case was enshrined in the statute book by the political class during the N.D.A. rule.

This provision for providing special protection to higher bureaucracy and those above them was readily adopted by the State governments also through the route of executive orders.

As a counterpart of the CBI which deals with complaints of corruption against central government employees, the states also have their own anti-corruption agencies termed as Vigilance Bureaus to handle complaints of corruption against public servants. Similar executive orders are in place for the state vigilance bureaus to seek prior permission of the state government before initiating enquiry and investigation against the civil servants employed with state. In case of the CBI, according to the executive order, now turned into law, it is required to seek prior permission in respect of enquiry against officers of the rank of joint secretary and above. In case of the state vigilance bureaus, they are required to secure prior permission for enquiry and investigation against all gazetted officers.

As in the case of *Vineet Narain Vs Union of India* discussed above, an enterprising Chief of Bihar State Vigilance Bureau- DP Ojha-known for his crusading zeal against crime and corruption, challenged the executive order requiring prior permission in Patna High Court. In this case, ***DP Ojha Vs State of Bihar*** (Cr.WJC No. 244 of 1999), the petitioner claimed that Vigilance Bureau being an investigation agency has statutory power under CrPC to make preliminary enquiry, register cases and carry an investigation on its own and the State government had no jurisdiction to put any restriction on it by issuing executive instructions. This challenged the order issued by Chief Secretary dated 7.2.83 to the effect that the Vigilance Bureau could not initiate any enquiry or close it on its own in respect of gazetted officers without the prior permission of the government through the Vigilance Commissioner. The Patna High Court accepted the contention of the petitioner and observed as follows : "The question is whether on completion of such preliminary enquiry, the Bureau is required to obtain a nod from the Vigilance Commissioner or the Chief Secretary, as the case may be before formally instituting the case ? The answer has to be in the negative. Requiring the Bureau to take any such permission would amount to impinging upon the jurisdiction of the investigating agency under Sections 154/156/157 CrPC and would be at a tangent with the provisions contained therein."

The above verdict of Patna High Court dated 2nd November 1999 clearly affirmed the stand of the Bihar Vigilance Bureau that no prior approval of the State Government was needed for enquiry and investigation into complaints of corruption against government officers. The State Government went in appeal before the Supreme Court against the judgement of Patna High Court. The concerned criminal Appeal No. 26 of 2001 (*State of Bihar Vs DP Ojha)* was dismissed by the Supreme Court which upheld the judgement of Patna High Court on this issue. The Supreme Court observed: "We find that the judgment is based upon the decision of this court in *Vineet Narain Vs Union of India* reported in 1998 (i) SCC 226. Thus the point involved in this appeal is covered by the said judgement and we are in agreement with the view expressed therein. We, thus, see no reasons to interfere. The appeal stands dismissed ...." This judgement is dated 20 February 2003.

Thus the highest judiciary of the country has twice invalidated any curb on the powers of the investigating agencies (CBI and State vigilance Bureaus) in investigating complaints of corruption against public servants. That clearly points to the evident flaw in the existing anti corruption mechanism of the country against which Anna's movement was directed and which has rendered the mechanism largely ineffective in curbing corruption.

The provisions regarding prior permission or sanction for investigating and prosecuting the corrupt public servants are arbitrary and unjustified on two counts. First, the distinction sought to be made between the offences of corruption and general crime like murder, dacoity, theft, etc., is entirely incorrect. If no prior permission or sanction is required by police to investigate and prosecute a person accused of these offences, why should such a permission or sanction be required for investigating and prosecuting a public servant accused of corruption? To answer this question, one has to understand what exactly is ***"Crime".*** Criminologists agree that crime denotes "acts that are a violation of criminal laws of the country." According to **John Barron Mays**, "A crime is an offence against society. It consists in the commission of acts which have been legally proscribed." Another criminologist, **Clarence Darrow**, has defined crime as "act forbidden by the law of the land, and one which is considered sufficiently serious to warrant providing penalties for its commission."

In the light of this clear definition of the term "Crime", corruption of public servants is as much a crime as murder, dacoity, theft etc. For it is clubbed together with other conventional crimes mentioned above in the criminal law of India. The Indian Penal code enacted in the 19th Century enlisted corruption in the form of bribery as an offence like any other and prescribed punishment for it vide sections 161 to 165. This was further elaborated and specified in the Prevention of Corruption Act. In a sense, corruption is a more serious crime than ordinary or conventional crimes. For conventional crimes cause harm to individuals, that is, to the particular victims of crimes, while corruption adversely affects the whole society. There is no justification at all in putting a brake on the process of investigation and prosecution of corrupt public servants by executive orders.

Secondly, there is no justification for making a distinction between higher and lower public servants in the matter of investigation and prosecution for corrupt practices. Public servants of the rank of joint secretary and above in Central Government and gazetted officers in State Governments have been protected by provisions for prior permission and sanction under the existing system, while clerks and patwaries are not. Apart from being patently unfair and iniquitous, this invidious and arbitrary distinction between joint secretary/gazetted officer and clerk/patwari makes the anti-corruption system stand on its head. It is not only unwarranted but verges on absurdity. The Indian Penal Code does not make any distinction between crime committed by a higher dignitary and that by a lowly person. Why should the governments-central and state-make such a distinction in respect of corruption which is a big crime that corrodes the whole society?

13

CBI: The Kingpin of Anti-corruption Mechanism

The biggest drawback of the existing anti-corruption regime is that its operating arm-the CBI is totally under the thumb of the political party in power. Although constituted as a specialist police unit with statutory powers to register and investigate cases of corruption against central government employees, it has come to be just a department of the central government under complete control of the government in power. Legally, it is empowered under Section 154, 156 and 157 Cr PC to register a case and investigate into incidence of corruption on its own, which is a semi-judicial function. But in actual practice, it goes about its job only after a nod from the government department under which it is placed. Right from the stage of the appointment of its Chief - the Director - to the process of investigation, the CBI is controlled by the government in power almost from day to day.

A glaring example of the central government's interference in the functioning of CBI came to light in the infamous *fodder s c am case* of Bihar. It was entirely due to the vigilant eye of higher judiciary - the Patna High Court and Supreme Court - that the CBI could complete the investigation and file charge sheets in the concerned cases against former Chief Minister Laloo Prasad Yadav and others in June 1997, but not without hiccups due to pulls and pressures to derail the investigation by the United Front Government at the center of which Laloo Prasad's RJD was a part. In June 1997 itself, the CBI Director, Joginder Singh was transferred out of CBI. And, there was also a move to transfer Upen Biswas, the regional director of CBI, who was guiding the investigation under the close watch of Patna High Court.

Even with the regime change at the center, Laloo Prasad's clout with the central government continued, except during the period of the NDA government. His RJD party emerged as a major partner of the first UPA government which came to power after 2004 parliamentary election. Laloo Prasad flourished as a powerful Railway minister for full five years until the rout of his party in 2009 parliamentary elections, even as he was facing multiple charges of corruption in courts of Bihar and Jharkhand. This is the irony of our electoral laws which shall be dealt with at some length in a later chapter.

In the meantime, as he was presiding over the empire of the railway ministry, Laloo Prasad was on trial in a case of disproportionate assets launched against him in course of fodder scam investigations. It was a strong case, as made out by CBI earlier, but when Laloo Prasad became a part of the UPA-I government, the CBI became lukewarm about it in course of the trial. As a result, the case ended in acquittal in sessions court. Although CBI denied any negligence on its part in pursuing the case properly in court, the cat was out of the bag when the question of filing an appeal in the High Court against the acquittal came up. The CBI blatantly refused to file an appeal against the judgement which it normally does in such cases. And when the State Government filed an appeal in the High Court, it was pleaded on behalf of Laloo Prasad that the CBI alone was competent to file an appeal.

This is one of the numerous instances in which CBI keeps on tight-rope walking in investigation and prosecution of cases of corruption against political functionaries to suit the interest of the party in power. It could be in the form of going slow in investigation or delaying and prolonging the trial on one pretext or another or soft-peddling the prosecution case in course of trial or facilitating the release on bail of the accused by not opposing it and numerous other ways. Here again the case against Laloo Prasad pending trial in law courts illustrates the point. By May 2007, about 200 accused persons in fodder scam cases were convicted and sentenced to prison terms, but the trial of cases in which Laloo Yadav figures as accused was allowed to languish as long as he remained in power during UPA. I regime. The fate and duration of the trial against him, thus, depended upon the clout he enjoyed with the central government by virtue of the strength of his party in Parliament.

That brings out the major institutional drawback in dealing with corruption charges against politicians in power as long as the CBI remains under the control of the government. The remedy lies in placing the CBI under the control of an independent semi-judicial authority to enable it to carry on with investigation and prosecution in cases of corruption without interference by any central government department, directly or indirectly. The proposed institution of Lokpal ideally fits into the bill. The CBI can perform its task in investigating and prosecuting corruption cases impartially and expeditiously only if it is placed squarely under lokpal. That would remove a major hurdle in curbing corruption in high quarters.

The malfunctioning of the CBI under pulls and pressures of the government in *power has been best* brought out by an insider, B.R. Lall, a former Joint Director of *CBI.* In his highly revealing book," who owns CBI: The Naked Truth" Lall has unmasked the flip flop of the then CBI Director Joginder Singh to serve the interests of his political bosses. In the Jharkhand Mukti Morcha Bribery case, the Director asked the S.P. Arun Sinha who was investigating the case to conclude the case in a particular way and collect evidence accordingly. "Arun Sinha, the S.P., confided in me later," writes Lall, "that Joginder Singh had asked him to change the case diary and a material statement and on his refusal to oblige, he was sent to Silchar from where he came back under court orders". The main accused in J.M.M. Bribery case, it may be noted, was P.V. Narsimha Rao, the congress President, on whom the government of Devegowda was dependent for political support.

"Continuing the same way", writes Lall, "Joginder Singh extended protection to the family members of Narsimha Rao in the Urea Case. He ordered post-haste transfer of R.M Singh, the D.I.G. supervising the case, who was camping at Hyderabad and was likely to come heavy on the family members of former P.M." Similarly, in the Lakhubhai Pathak case, the Law Minister sent a letter conveying government decision not to oppose the bail petition of the accused. The letter was handed over to the CBI counsel Gopal Subramaniam who refused to oblige. He opposed the bail petition and, being disgusted, walked out of the case afterwards.

The vagaries of the CBI, dancing to the tune of its political masters, was well illustrated in its handling of the Fodder scam cases. For people of Bihar, it was no secret that the then CBI Director was doing everything to side-track or derail the investigation under pressure from the incumbent Prime Minister Devegowda, For Laloo Prasad was very much a part of the ruling Janata Dal. It was whispered in political circles in Bihar that the Chief Minister of Bihar, Laloo Prasad, was collecting funds through the Fodder Scam to finance the next election of the Janata Dal then in power at the center, As long as Devegowda was the P.M., whom the Director had gone out of his way to cultivate, Joginder singh was not only soft pedalling the investigation of cases against the Bihar Chief Minister, but holding the view that no case was made out against Laloo Prasad. That was the bone of contention between him and U.N. Biswas, the Joint Director, who was guiding the investigation under orders of the Patna High Court. The Director even tried to transfer U.N. Biswas, as mentioned earlier, but failed because the Patna High Court set its foot down to scuttle the move.

But once Devegowda was out and I.K. Gujral succeeded him, the Director changed his track. May be, he tried to build the same kind of rapport with Gujral as he had done with Devegowda but failed. Mean while, there was a great hype in the media about the involvement of Bihar Chief Minister and other big wigs in the Fodder Scam cases. The Patna High Court was pursuing the cases relentlessly and following the investigation closely from date to date. Being very media savvy and having lost his connect with I.K. Gujral, the incumbent Prime Minister, the Director took an about turn in his view on the scam cases. Whereas he had earlier held that no case was made out against the Bihar Chief Minister, he made a somersault by June 1997 by agreeing with his Joint

Director U.N. Biswas and approving filing of charge sheet against Laloo Prasad and others in Fodder Scam cases.

What followed was nothing short of a dramatic interlude. Here is the Director Joginder Singh's take on the developments following his approval of the charge sheet. In his book "Inside CBI". which he got published in 1999 (Chandrika Publications), he writes: "I attended a meeting with the Prime Minister on June 18, 1997. The meeting was also attended by N.N vohra, who was resurrected nearly three years after retirement, as officer on Special Duly in P.M.O. Also present was Mr. T.S. Satish Chandran, the Principal Secretary to the P.M. Vohra said that I should send a faxstating that Chief Minister Laloo Prasad Yadav would not; be arrested. I said that I would not do that unless the government gave the order to me in writing". And further, "when Gujral's Principal Secretary approached me to save the then Chief Minister of Bihar, I had no doubt that he was only carrying his superior's orders. I found the plea put forward by him (that there would be bloodshed if the Bihar Chief Minister was arrested) unbelievable and hilarious."

The tussle between the C.B.I. Director and the Central Government continued-the former insisting on a written order for not arresting the Chief Minister and the government persisting with verbal instruction. In course of this stalemate, the Director met the Prime Minister and what transpired between them is best described by Joginder Singh in his book. He writes: "I met Mr. Gujral on June 20 at about 5.20 P.M and told him that his wishes could not be complied with since the Home Ministry had not sent any official assessment on potential disturbances in Bihar if the Chief Minister was arrested by the CBI............. Almost in fit of rage he said, 'You cannot control Your Joint Director (meaning U.N. Biswas). I said, Sir, he is only carrying out the direction of Patna High Court. I cannot and will not tell him not to do his duty."

The matter rested there until the Chief Minister of Bihar Laloo Prasad and other co-accused were charge-sheeted in court by the CBI on 23 June, 1997. His anticipatory bail petition was rejected by the Patna High Court and his appeal against the High Court order was also rejected by the Supreme Court on 29 July 1997. The next day he was arrested by Bihar Police and later remanded to judicial custody. Nothing happened in Bihar by way of disturbance or bloodshed, as assiduously made out by the Home Ministry, evidently at the instance of the ruling Janata Dal party to stall the arrest of Laloo Prasad.

That was only a glimpse of how CBI is checkmated at every step and made to dance to the tune of the central government interfering in the process of investigation from behind the scene. It is intriguing and ominous that the government in power should resort to this kind of manipulation to influence the process of investigation by the CBI. In Vineet Narain Vs. Union of India, the Supreme court had clarified that the term "Superintendence" occurring in section 4(1) of the Delhi Special Police Establishment Act, 1946 has to be construed in a manner consistent with other provisions of the Act and general statutory powers of investigation. The "general statutory powers" vesting in the investigating agency are provided by sections 154, 156 and 157 Cr PC. The above provisions of the Cr PC do not allow any interference with the course of investigation, not even by the court.

It was in the background of the above kind of covert or indirect interference in the process of investigation that the eminent jurist Falil S. Nariman observed that CBI was functioning under successive central governments "not by notes on files but on nods or winks". (as noted in an article, "Erosion of credibility; need to insulate CBI from, Political control" by Shanker Sen, in 'the Tribune', Chandigarh dated 28 January 2011). The issue of making CBI a worthwhile institution for fighting corruption by freeing it from political control has been raised from time to time at various levels. Shanker Sen, an eminent police professional, ex-chief of National Police Academy and currently Senior Fellow, Institute of Social sciences, New Delhi, observes: "Strong political will is needed to make the CBI independent, a - political and effective".

A more forthright suggestion was made by B.R. Lall, ex-joint Director, CBI, at a conference of CBI, Chiefs of anti-corruption Bureaus of States and central Psu's at Delhi in November 1996. In his book referred to earlier, he writes: "I suggested that the CBI be placed under the charge of an independent Board, so that it could function impartially and truthfully, independent of the government (whom it was supposed to investigate) .... That this Board should exercise all the powers which were vested in the government."

In an interview given to Journalist Rudroneel Ghosh, Justice V.N. Khare, former Chief Justice of the Supreme Court of India, has said, among other things, that if the CBI is under the government and the government is the prosecutor, there is a clear conflict of interest in prosecuting government corruption and, therefore, the CBI should be autonomous in any case. His interview is reported in The Times of India, Patna dated 30 December, 2011.

14

Ombudsman in Different Countries

The idea of Lokpal was derived from the institution of Ombudsman already in place in different countries of the world. Historically, the origin of Ombudsman can he traced back to the setting up of this institution in the 18th century in Sweden by the King, Charles XII. The Ombudsman established by the king was primarily to ensure correct conduct of royal officials. The institution evolved further during the 19th century when it was incorporated in the Swedish Constitution and its duties were formally defined. It was constituted as a parliamentary body to supervise the functioning of government officials for ensuring their compliance with laws and regulations. The significance of this institution was that for the first time a constitutional watchdog was established to oversee the working of government officials including judges.

The institution of Ombudsman caught up and developed more fully during the 20th Century particularly in the wake of the Second World War. Interestingly, this coincided with the adoption of specific anti-corruption legislation in India in the aftermath of the Second World War. It was in this period that about a hundred countries across the world established their own version of ombudsman with varying duties and responsibilities depending upon their historical, political and social background.

Originating from Sweden, the first Ombudsman institution outside Sweden was established in Finland when it became independent of Russia in 1918. The other Nordic countries like Norway and Denmark followed suit and set up their own institutions of ombudsman. It soon spread to all European countries and subsequently to the whole world. In U.K, it is formally referred to as the Parliamentary Commissioner, that is, the United Kingdom Parliamentary Commission for Administration.

In fact, New Zealand was the fourth country after Sweden, Finland and Denmark to establish the office of ombudsman in 1962. To start with, the New Zealand Ombudsman's jurisdiction was limited to investigating complaints about Central Government departments and organisations. But in 1975, the Ombudsman's jurisdiction was extended to include local government agencies also.

In Britain, the office of Parliamentary Commissioner for Administration was created in 1967 covering the affairs of the central government departments. As the name indicates, the British ombudsman is a parliamentary institution attached to the British Parliament and usually investigates complaints referred to it by members of parliament. As such, additional posts of ombudsman are in place attached to the Scottish parliament, Welsh Assembly and Northern Ireland Assembly. Apart from territorial bifurcation, there is functional separation also, as specific national health service ombudsman was subsequently created to look into complaints regarding the nationalised health service. It may be noted that provisions of necessary health service to every citizens is a very important function of the Government in Britain and any compliant in this regard is to be looked into by the ombudsman.

Although the functions and jurisdictions of ombudsman vary from country to country, the institution in some form or the other has come to be established in most parts of the world. In 1995 the European Union created the post of an European ombudsman. The institution has become global. As of now, around 140 countries of the world have ombudsman type institutions in place as a correctional mechanism in their system of governance. The general ombudsman covers all spheres of governmental activities, but there is also a specialised type ombudsman that deals with only specific area of governance like the British health service ombudsman.

The common denominator of ombudsman in most countries is its function as a grievance redressal institution. As such, it looks into citizen's complaints about actions and decisions of government departments and agencies with varying degrees of power of enforcement of its findings. It provides a check on governmental activities in the interest of the citizen and overseas the investigation of complaints of improper government activity against the citizens. If the compliant is substantiated, further redressal of the citizens grievance depends upon the laws of the country concerned. It is largely an individual citizens oriented institution which seeks to resolve their complaints against the state administration. But it is also authorised to check and detect inefficiencies, malpractices and violations of law on its own imitative. In many countries, the jurisdiction of ombudsman extends beyond dealing with alleged mal-administration to promoting and protecting human rights. In such cases, the ombudsman is recognized as the national human rights institution.

It is evident from the above that corruption as such has not been the main focus of attention of ombudsman in most countries, unless, of course, corruption is taken in its wider meaning of moral degeneration, decomposition or malfunctioning in general. In its restricted meaning, corrupt practice like bribery, corruption was not much of a problem in the Scandinavian countries where the institution of ombudsman originated. Large scale governmental corruption-administrative and political as in the case of India, has neither been a major issue in the other western countries where the institution of ombudsman came to be established. In this connection, it may be remembered that in Transparency International's corruption perceptions index, India was ranked 87th out of 178 counties in 2010. A 2005 study conducted by Transparency International in India found that more than 55 per cent of people in the country had first hand experience of paying bribes or influence peddling to get jobs done in the public offices. In contrast, the situation in western countries is much different in respect of plain bribery and corruption from that prevailing in India. The contrast has become sharper, as in 2011 Transparency International's Corruption Perception Index, India slipped to a low 95 among 183 countries of the world.

In the circumstances, the ombudsman model of western countries is hardly of much use in tackling the corruption situation in India. The Indian institution of Lokpal which is meant to combat the gigantic problem of governmental corruption has to evolve its own format and modality. The only thing the Lokpal movement has borrowed from the Ombudsman model of European countries is the concept of an independent authority or institution to oversee the functioning of government in general.

As regards protection and promotion of human rights, which Ombudsman is supposed to do in many countries, India already has a high profile National Human Rights Commission at the Central level. Since it is inception, it has been headed by a retired chief Justice of the Supreme Court with a fixed tenure. Many of the states have also set up their own Human Rights Commissions to deal with complaints of human rights violation at the state level. These are in the nature of grievance redressal institutions.

Similarly, in respect of territorial ombudsman, as in the case of Britain, a majority of the states in India have established ombudsman type of institutions termed as Lokayuktas. The powers, functions and jurisdiction of state Lokayuktas vary form state to state. The Lokayuktas are constituted by state governments which define their duties and responsibilities. So far, 18 states gave got the institution of Lokayukta in place and recently Uttarakhand has become the 19th State to opt for its own Lokayukta with wide powers. Incidentally Anna team has fully endorsed the Uttarakhand model of Lokayukta as a fit instrument of fighting corruption.

There is, however, nothing much to talk about the record of state Lokayuktas on the anti-corruption front except for a few states. In some states, they have been busy dealing with arrears of pension and such other minor concerns of citizens rather than investigating and initiating action against corrupt public servants. The Lokayuktas of two states Karnataka and UP have proved to be exceptions, of course, in recent times. In Karnataka, the Chief Minister and in UP a Minister had to quit on charges of corruption at the instance of their respective Lokayuktas. In another state, Gujarat, the appointment of Lokayukta by the Governor without consultation with the incumbent Chief Minister has itself become controversial.

In any case, the institutions of the state Lokayukta as an anti-corruption agency has nothing much to show or enthuse about. In absence of political will on the part of state governments which appoint the Lokayuktas, the institution has proved to be non-starter in the fight against corruption, specially at the higher level. At best, the institution of Lokayukta in state has come up as a grievance redressel agency rather than an anti-corruption one. Since the main focus of Lokpal movement is on fighting against corruption, there is substance in Anna teams demand for model lokayukta institution to be established in all states with enough power and jurisdiction to curb corruption at the state level.

15

Electoral Reforms

As J.P. earlier, Anna Hazare emerged as the flag bearer of anti-corruption crusade in India in the 21st Centaury. J.P. was a giant of the freedom struggle and a nation builder par excellence in the tradition of Mahatma Gandhi and Jawaharlal Nehru. His anti corruption crusade was only a part of his call for "*total revolution* "which had a much wider dimension and encapsuled sweeping socio-political reforms. There is therefore , no question of trying to compare J.P's movement with Anna's campaign against corruption. But, like J.P. again, Anna and his team are talking about such electoral reforms as right to recall elected representatives and right to reject corrupt candidates at elections.

Right to recall of elected representatives was also a plank of J.P's movement but only as a part of his call for a total overhaul of the political system. It was more a part of his move to strengthen the democratic rights of the people than that of his anti-corruption crusade. The right to recall is an old concept which has been brought up and debated in democratic countries world over at some time or the other. In India also it was thought of and debated but has not been found to be practicable on the ground. In any case, it has not been taken up seriously by any political party in India, either the ruling or opposition, so far. Neither is it likely to be, for it bristles with practical difficulties in implementation on the ground.

But there is one agenda of electoral reform which needs to be adressed urgently in order to prevent criminalisation of politics. This relates to disqualification for membership of Parliament and

State legislatures of tainted politicians with criminal background. Since corruption is also a crime, legally and ethically, the disqualification of criminal elements also means disqualification of the corrupt.

There is nothing new about the concept of disqualification. A whole Chapter (Chapter-III) of the Representation of the Peoples Act, as amended up to 1992, is devoted to disqualification of persons from being members of Parliament and State legislatures. Section 8, sub section (3) of the Act debars a person "convicted of any offence and sentenced to imprisonment for not less than two years" from being a legislator. That would cover those convicted and sentenced to imprisonment for two years and more for bribery and corruption also under the Prevention of Corruption Act, as in the case of any other offence like murder, dacoity, rape etc.

If this provision could be effective, it could prevent the entry of crime and corrsuption tainted persons into the temples of democracy - the Parliament and State legislatures. But the disqualification envisaged in this clause of the Representation of the Peoples Act. is not effective for two reasons First, the disqualification is operative only after a person has been tried and convicted by a court of law and not until then. Limiting the disqualification to conviction has made it totally ineffective. The ground reality is that investigation of offences, particularly in case of powerful and resourceful offenders, often takes years and trial by a court of law much longer to complete. The infamous fodder scam cases against powerful politicians of Bihar, for instance, are pending trial for over a decade and there is no sign of the trial concluding early. Meanwhile, the politicians on trial continue to be "hon'ble" members of legislatures and Parliament and even flourish as ministers.

In a situation where thousands of criminal cases are pending in trial and appellate courts across the country, bringing the criminal justice system to the breaking point, litmus test of conviction allows crime and corruption tainted persons ample scope to nullify the disqualification provision. In case of some notorious mafia leaders of the coal belt of Eastern India, about 20 heinous crimes like murder, extortions, etc., remained pending trial for around 20 years, during which they merrily entered the concerned legislature and carried on with their brand of politics. Our legal system is such that an accused can manage to prolong trial on one technical ground or another for ages.

The second and more crippling provision of the disqualification clause is its non-operation even after conviction until the deposal of appeal filed by the convicted person. Sub Section 4 of Section 8 of the Representation of the Peoples Act lays down "Not with standing anything, a disqualification in either sub section shall not, in the case of a person who, on the date of the conviction is a member of Parliament or the legislature of a state, take effect until three months have elapsed from that date or, if within that period an appeal or application for revision is brought up in respect of the conviction or the sentence, *until that appeal or application is disposed* by the court." This proviso conveniently and unobtrusively robs the disqualification provision of whatever little meaning it had.

This is not a hypothetical scenario. A 1994 newspaper report about the member of a state Assembly serving life imprisonment in a case of mass murder runs as follows "Mr... is allegedly a history - sheeter involved in a number of criminal cases and serving jail imprisonment following life term by the court for his involvement in a massacre of nine persons about 10 years ago. Mr.... has however been allowed by the higher court to attend the proceedings of the assembly from jail following his appeal against the judgement of the law court". (The Times of India Patna edition, 2 July 1994. This is a telling example of the appeal proviso in operation. It makes a mockery of the entire disqualification provision meticulously enshrined in Section 8 of the Representation of the people Act. It is a typical case of the left hand taking away what the right hand gives, a play of the tokenism which the political class has perfected into a fine art.

The issue of criminalisation of politics and electoral reforms to curb it has long been under discussion at various levels. Successive Chief Election Commissioners have come out with proposals for electoral reforms to put a check on the malady of criminalization of politics. The government appointed Vohra committee had also gone into the problem and made some valuable recommendations. The stage of discussion and interaction with different agencies and organs of government has long been over. It was time now to adopt concrete legal measures to put a stop to the cancerous growth of criminalisation which is threatening the body politic of the country. If the government and the political class as a whole has the will, a simple amendment in the Representation of the People Act can put a check on this growing menace.

Towards this end, sub sections 3 and 4 of Section 8 of the Act should be deleted. And a sub section should be added debarring a person from being a member of parliament and state legislatures against whom a competent court has taken cognizance of a criminal offence for trial. The disqualification should start from the moment a court of law takes cognizance of criminal offence and summons the accused persons for trial.

In case of sitting legislators, if cognizance of criminal offence committed by them is taken by a court of law and they are summoned for trial, they should be suspended from the legislature (that is, not allowed to participate in the proceedings and vote but to continue to draw salary) until acquitted after trial. On conviction by the first court, they should be disqualified without waiting for the result of the appeal, if any. If acquittal is obtained on appeal, the disqualification should be set aside.

It must be clarified that disqualifying persons from contesting elections just after a court takes cognizance of charge sheet against them and summons them for trial does not mean pronouncing them guilty before completion of trial. They will continue to be deemed innocent until convicted by court after due trial and enjoy all rights and privileges of a citizen, *except the right to contest elections and be members of state legislatures and parliament.* This exception is necessary because cognizance of a criminal offence against them by a competent court after judicial scrutiny of the charge sheet submitted by the investigating agency does create reasonable suspicion about their involvement. And those entering the highest organs of democratic polity should, like Caesar's wife, be above suspicion. What is proposed is an extraordinary remedy for an extraordinary situation or ailment. Of all the measures of electoral reforms being suggested and discussed at diverse forums, this is one single step that can bring about a significant and qualitative change for a better and cleaner functioning democracy. For Anna's anti corruption crusaders, it is much better to push for this vital and attainable electoral reform than to chase the mirage of reforms like right to recall and right to reject. No major country in the world has the right to recall at the national level in its statute book.

In the USA, many states at the local level have incorporated the right to recall in their respective constitutions, but no such provision has been made in the American Constitution at the national level. It may be remembered that, as the name itself indicates, the United States of America is a conglomeration of 50 different states, which have their own separate constitutions and laws. In a similar background, only one province of Canada provides for the right to recall. Even in a tiny country in comparison to India, like Switzerland, only six cantons, equivalent to our districts, have empowered their citizens with the right to recall.

In a big country like India, where the electorate of a parliamentary constituency comprises around a million voters with multiple loyalties of caste, creed etc. right to recall is quite impractible. In fact, it may create many problems instead of solving any. On the other hand, the simple agenda of electoral reform aimed at prevention of criminalisation as suggested above, can be more effective in cleaning up of our political system. For criminalization of politics in the conventional sense is as much an ailment of our democratic polity as corruption in its commonly understood meaning. In fact conventional crimes and corruption are two sides of the same coin. Just as the institution of Lokpal is necessary to curb corruption, electoral reform is necessary to check the growing menace of criminalisation of politics. For, if corruption is a form of crime in legal sense, crime in its conventional meaning is the worst form of corruption in moral sense.

16

The Cause Betrayed

The tide of Lokpal movement started by Anna Hazare in April 2011 ebbed and waned by the end of December 2011 without the institution of Lokpal coming into being. The marathon but rambling debate over the issue of Lokpal kept the people of India, the middle classes actually, engrossed with the hope of a meaningful institution coming up to check the growing menace of corruption. Anna's catalystic movement had aroused the people in general, long reconciled to co-exist with wide spread corruption, to feel the need and urge for an end to multilayered corruption corroding the country. But at the end of the day, as the year 2011 was consigned to the ashtray of history, people's hopes were dimmed, if not altogether extinguished, about the emergence of a meaningful ombudsman to oversee and keep in check the erring and rapacious wielders of power.

What went wrong ? To answer that, one has to begin with the nature of the protracted debating exercise over the issue indulged in by the political class. The lead player in this game of one-upmanship was, of course, the UPA government and its political trumpeteers. The moment the little known anti-corruption crusader from Ralegan Siddhi-Anna Hazare-brought up the issue of Lokpal as the prime agenda of the country, the stalwarts of the government stood up to deflate his movement. While P.M. Manmohan Singh, the show piece of UPA government, kept saying sweet words about Anna and promising to bring the institution of Lokpal, his political colleagues went about denigrating Anna's movement with unconcealed ire, if not venom. That resulted in some sort of an adversary relationship between the anti-corruption crusaders and the government.

One common point repeatedly made by government spokesmen was that Lokpal Bill could be enacted only in parliament and not in street, referring to Anna's movement. It was utterly misleading and wrong to condemn Anna's anti-corruption crusaders on this score because they never challenged the exclusinve power of Parliament to enact laws. They were agitating on the street only to convey their concern against all pervasive corruption to Parliament and present before it their version of an effective Lokpal Bill. What was wrong with that ? It is the common people who elect members of Parliament to make laws and they have every right to demand enactment of effective laws to check corruption. It is the people, the electors, who are the masters of Parliament and not the other way about.

Another misconceived notion spread by the political class was that the Lokpal was in the nature of a super government or parallel center of power which could be a threat to our Parliamentary democracy. No handpicked body of wise men could be allowed to challenge the supremacy of a popularly elected government. No one disputed that, definitely not the anti-corruption crusaders who led the movement for Lokpal. The phantom of Lokpal as a leviathan out to supplant or supersede the elected government was entirely a figment of imagination. It was on the basis of their misconception that in the re-introduced Lokpal Bill, the government provided for reservation in the composition of multi-member Lokpal in terms of caste and creed. As if Lokpal was a milch cow or a power center bestowing largesse's on the people to be shared by diverse castes and creeds.

Nothing could be more incorrect or misconceived than that. The simple fact is that the concept of Lokpal is that of a watchdog to keep an eye on those political power-wielders and bureaucrats who were apt to indulge in corrupt practices at the cost of the common people. It may be noted here, as mentioned in an earlier chapter, that the very idea of such a watchdog or ombudsman originated and was successfully implemented in the North European Countries which are epitomes of practicing democracy. To project

Lokpal as an all powerful Leviathan out to usurp the power of governance was either sheer naivety or deliberate attempt to confuse the issue.

The majority of government functionaries who were by and large above board had nothing to be scared about Lokpal. It is those among the powerful higher bureaucracy, the so-called "decision-makers" and their political bosses, who were worried over coming up of a meaningful institution of Lokpal, Unduly protected by the provisions of "previous sanction" and "prior permission" in the existing anti-corruption laws, it is this class which would feel exposed to investigation into corruption charges against them. Because these safety provisions of "previous sanction" and "prior permission" would have no place in Lokpal.

It would be relevant in this connection to note that according to the latest rating released by Hongkong-based Political and economical Risk consultancy Limited, the Indian bureaucracy ranks the lowest in the index of corruption and harassment of industrial entrepreneurs in Asia. It ranks well below Vietnam, Indonesia, Philippines and China. It is this class of bureaucrats and their political god-fathers who felt threatened by Lokpal and raised the bogey of a parallel power centre in it. In raising this false alarm to stall the creation of Lokpal, they were looking in a dark night for a black cat which was not there.

Coming to the Lokpal Bill presented by the government in Parliament at the end of December 2011, passed in Lok Sabha, it epitomises nothing but an exercise in futility. A typical example of tokenism resorted to by governments from time to time to mollify people's sentiments without actually giving or conceding anything.

The Lokpal, as envisaged in the government Bill passed by Lok Sabha in December 2011, was so hedged in by restrictions as to make it virtually a paper tighter.

First the Lokpal may have an enquiry wing, but no power to investigate into corruption charges and carry the investigation to its logical conclusion on its own. It could conduct preliminary enquiry into cases of corruption but would have to send its enquiry report to Central Vigilance Commission. The CVC would examine the report and send it back to Lokpal with its own comments. If the Lokpal so decides, it would send it to CBI for investigation. The CBI, a fully government controlled agency, would investigate the case on its own and apprise the Lokpal with its findings or conclusion for final approval.

This circulatory movement of corruption complaint from Lokpal to CVC, back to Lokpal, onwards to CBI and back to Lokpal would not only act as a clog in the wheel of investigation but would adversely impact the process and quality of investigation itself. While the complaint keeps moving along the labyrinthian course, the person under enquiry would have ample time and scope to try and extricate himself from the charge of corruption. In fact, this entire provision seems to have been made in order to provide full opportunity to the corrupt to escape from the purview of Lokpal.

In this respect, the Lokpal as envisaged by government, would not have the power of even of a Sub Inspector of Police who has full power to register a case and carry on investigation on complaint of corruption against any one. Under sections 154 to 157 Cr PC, the officer in-charge of a police station is authorised or rather duty bound to enquire and investigate into complaints about any cognizable offence committed by any one. And, as discussed in an earlier Chapter, corruption punishable by law under IPC or Prevention of Corruption Act is as much an offence as murder, dacoity, theft etc. In the light of this undisputed legal position, the circumlocutory procedure prescribed for handling complaints of corruption by Lokpal in the government Bill made a mockery not only of the process of investigation but of the institution of Lokpal itself.

Secondly, even this restricted role of Lokpal, as envisaged in the government Bill, would be confined to complaints against group A and group B officers only. In respect of group C and D government employees, complaint of corruption would be sent to the CVC which alone would have the jurisdiction to deal with it. It baffles all logic to conceive of this arbitrary splitting up of the practitioners of corruption into groups A B and C D for the purpose of investigation. The ground reality is that in any number of cases, government functionaries from both groups A B and C D - are jointly involved in transactions of corruption. What would happen in such cases ? This bifurcation into groups A B on the one hand and C D on the other is not only impracticable but verges on absurdity. Law does not make any distinction between high and low in regard to practitioners of corruption.

At this stage, it would be relevant to examine the position of the CVC itself as an anti-corruption agency. It is not generally known that this much trumpeted government controlled agency is as much a toothless organisation as the government proposed Lokpal. It can "inquire or cause an inquiry or investigation to be made" into any complaint against members of all India services, group A officers of the Central government and employees of public sector under taking. On receipt of the enquiry report the CVC would advise the central government or the Public sector under taking concerned about further course of action. The central government or the P.S.U. concerned "shall consider the advise of the commission and take appropriate action". But where the central government or the concerned P.S.U. "does not agree with the advice of the commission, it shall, for reasons to be recorded in writing, communicate the same to the commission." (Proviso to Section 17(3) of the Central Vigilance Commission Act, 2003). Here again what the right hand gives, the left hand takes away. The parent organisation of the officer under enquiry - the central government or the P.S.U. concerned is free to disagree with the advice of the CVC and reject it, "for reasons to be recorded in writing".

The CVC is thus a mere advisory body and its advice is not binding on the government or the employer of persons under enquiry. On top of that, it has no enquiry or investigation wing of its own. It only gets enquiry into corruption charges made by internal Vigilance agencies of the government and Public Sector under takings and offers its advice to them. How can such a handicapped organisation deal with large scale corruption involving group C and D employees ? It is obvious that the entire exercise of artificial division between groups A B and C D for the purpose of enquiry into corruption charges was aimed at cutting the proposed Lokpal to size.

And the biggest blow to the institution of Lokpal as envisaged in the government Bill was to keep the CBI out of its control. In a typically Orwellian manner of double speak, the government Bill allowed the Lokpal to have the power of "superintendence and direction" over CBI only in respect of matters referred to it by Lokpal. And the Lokpal would not exercise its power to require the CBI to investigate a case in a particular manner. Thus, under the government Bill, CBI, the master key to unlock the citadel of corruption, remained fully under the control of the government or political party in power.

It may be noted that a wide spectrum of legal luminaries, anti-corruption crusaders and police professionals, apart from political parties other than the ruling, have been pleading for freeing the CBI from octopus-like grip of politicians in power. And for placing it under an independent board or instituion so that it could parform its task for which it was meant without fear or favour. A common complaint of opposition political parties has been that the ruling party used or misused the CBI to serve its partisan political interest. The obvious solution was to put this premier anti-corruption institution under the control and superintendence of an independent semi judicial authority.The best option was to put it under an independent watchdog institution like Lokpal. That, would have not only demolished the oft-repeated charge of misuse of CBI by the government but also provided the Lokpal with an effective instrument to curb corruption. In fact, Lokpal without the working arm of CBI, would be like a gun without ammunition. But the government had other ideas.

The marathon debate on Lokpal, beginning April 2011, was not really about a weak Lokpal versus strong Lokpal. It was about a meaningful Lokpal or a meaningless Lokpal. And the government opted for the latter. That was the tragedy of the great Lokpal movement started by the little great Gandhian from Ralegam Siddhi - Anna Hazare. A great betroyal of a sacred cause by the political class.

17

2G Spectrum Scam

Even as Anna's raging and tearing stir for Lokpal came to a temporary stop, the dark shadow of the 2G Spectrum mega scam continued to haunt the corridors of power. Rumblings of gross irregularities and large scale corruption and bribery in 2G Spectrum allocation in 2008 were doing the rounds in opposition political circles, but the government had managed to keep it under carpet for two years. It was left to the institutional watchdog body like the Comptroller and Auditor General (CAG) to bell the cat and expose the mega scam. According to a report submitted by the CAG, based on money collected from 3G licenses, the loss to the government exchequer due to illicit under charging for licenses in 2008 was a whopping, Rupees *One lakh Seventy six thousand Three hundred Seventy nine Crores* (Rs. 1,76,379 Crores). The bribe money generated by such shady under charging was shared by big wigs of a major coalition partner of the U.P.A. government, concerned bureaucrats of Telecoms Department and others.

The exposure of such a big corruption story stunned the nation. The opposition cried foul. But, as usual, the ruling political establishment remained unfazed. The CAG exposure, however, was too big to be ignored any longer. Accordingly, the concerned Telecom Minister A. Raja of D.M.K. Party was made to resign and eventually landed in Tihar Jail pending CBI investigation. The famously honest Prime Minister brushed it off as compulsion of coalition politics.

But the cake was taken by the redoubtable Minister of P.M.'s own party who succeeded Raja as Telecom Minister. He came out with the astounding statement that zero loss or no loss to the government exchequer was caused due to spectrum allocation in 2008 by his predecessor. Persistent efforts on the part of government agencies to minimise the quantum of loss and belittle the loss assessment of the CAG continued. The Comptroller and Accountant General was called and questioned by the Parliamentary Committee on his findings, but he stuck to his assessment.

Meanwhile, the list of politicians and bureaucrats being accused in the case by CBI went on lengthening. In the process, the DMK Chief's daughter and prominent M.P. landed in prison. Subsequently, CBI also registered a case against the former Telecom Minister Dayanidhi Maran, his brother and Sun TV Managing Director Kalanidhi Maran, both belonging to DMK party, and a Malayasian billionaire T. Anand Krishnan, promoter of Maxis Communications of Malaysia. The CBI found that former Aircel Cheif C. Shivasankaran had been coerced by Dayanidhi Maran to sell off his company to Maxis Communications of Malaysia. Once the company was sold off by Shivasankaran to Maxis, the latter was given spectrum licenses. In return, Maxis bought shares in Maran brothers owned Sun TV worth Rs. 547 Crores at premium rates even though Sun TV did not have that kind of market value at that time.

Even as the government stalwarts continued to try and water down the scale of the scam, and some like the ruling party's new Telecom Minister referred to above even denying that there was a scam, an indefatigable political whistleblower - *Subramanium Swamy* - was hogging the headlines making wild allegarions against the leadership of both the congress party and its coalition partner DMK of having shared the bribe money generated by the scam. And in the surcharge milieu of Anna's anti-corruption movement, the allegation appeared to stick. That was more than enough to tarnish the sagging image of the U.P.A. government as corruption-ridden.

When rumblings about corruption in 2G Spectrum allocation surfaced in 2008, Subramanium Swamy had written to Prime Minister's Office on 29 November 2008 to sanction prosecution of the incumbent Telecom Minister A. Raza on corruption charges.

It may be noted that under section 19 of the Prevention of Corruption Act, 1988, prior sanction of the competent authority is necessary for prosecuting a 'Public Servant' (which includes a Minister also) on charges of corruption. And in the case of a central minister, Prime Minister is the competent authority to accord the required sanction. Since then, Swamy wrote four more letters to P.M.'s office to accord sanction. The P.M.'s office responded only after 16 months on 19 March 2010 rejecting Swamy's plea for according sanction. Swamy had moved the Supreme Court against the P.M.O.'s inaction on his letters for 16 months. Subsequently, Swamy petitioned the Supreme Court to issue guidelines for expediting sanction in such cases. The Court had reserved its judgment on Swamy's plea on 24 November 2010.

The long awaited judgment of the Supreme Court came on 31 January 2012 accepting Swamy's plea and giving categorical verdict on two counts. First, the court upheld the constitutional right of a citizen to lodge complaint regarding corruption against 'public servant' and observed that the petitioner had full right to seek P.M.'s sanction for prosecution of the then Telecom Minister. Second, and more importantly, the court held that required sanction under the Prevention of Corruption Act must be accorded within a period of four months. If the competent authority, in this case the Prime Minister, did not do so within four months, sanction would automatically be deemed to have been accorded.

This was a landmark verdict aimed at removing a major roadblock in speedy disposal of corruption cases against public servants. This is evident from the fact that a large number of corruption cases have remained pending for want of the required sanction of the competent authority. In response to the court's query, the Attorney General submitted that out of 319 cases referred to the central government for according sanction, 126 cases were pending. Evidently, that was in respect of Central Government employees. If the figure of cases against state governemnt employees pending for sanction is taken into account, the figure would be much higher.

Here is a telling example of how the mandatory provision of sanction for prosecution under section 19 of the Prevention of

Corruption Act can help a corrupt public servant to evade the arms of law and flourish. In connection with the notorious Fodder Scam of Bihar, the CBI had registered a case against the then treasury officer of Bhagalpur and others vide RC 63A/96 for fraudulent withdrawal of money from Bhagalpur treasury. After registration of the CBI case in 1996, the accused treasury office got himself transferred to Jharkhand. Since then, the CBI kept trying to obtain sanction for his prosecution and the matter kept hanging between the governments of Bihar and Jharkhand for *Six Years*. Meanwhile the accused treasury officer not only continued in service but also got promoted as Assistant Commissioner, Commercial tax department, and gracefully retired after reaching the age of superannuation. And, as a mockery, the long sought after mandatory sanction for prosecution was accorded by the Jharkhand government on 13 October 2011.

That would go to show how the provision of mandatory sanction under section 19 of Prevention of Corruption Act has acted as a protective shield for corrupt public servants to escape the clutches of law enforcing agencies. An unwarranted legacy of the colonial regime which enacted the original Prevention of corruption Act in 1947, this gaping loophole in the existing anti-corruption regime has already been dealt with in chapter 11. Suffice it to say that the Supreme Court has pronounced a remarkable verdict fixing a time limit of four months for according sanction for prosecution in cases of corruption. This should go a long way in curbing corruption by blocking the escape route of corrupt public servants through the connivance of their indulgent bosses. Provided the time limit is followed strictly by the central and state governments.

The Supreme Court has also suggested that appropriate amendment should be made in section 19 of prevention of corruption Act accordingly to set the time limit for according sanction. Evidently, until the law is amended, the time frame set by the highest court of the country should be strictly adhered to by all sanctioning authorities.

In fact, as discussed at some length in Chapter 11, this provision for mandatary sanction was a gift of the colonial regime to the bureaucracy which served as the pillar of the British rule. It was unfortunate that governments of independent India retained this provision for sanction which shielded the corrupt instead of exposing them to the rigours of law. If the anti-corruption regime of the country has to have any meaning, the provision for sanction should not only be amended by prescribing a time limit, as the Supreme Court has done, but deleted altogether from the prevention of corruption Act.

It would be relevant to note that the Anna's Jan Lokpal Bill has proposed the deletion of this provision altogether. According to it, once the Lokpal decided upon investigation into a corruption charge, there would be no need at all for any sanction for prosecution of the corrupt public servant. The government's Lokpal Bill introduced in Parliament also made a show of dispensing with the need for sanction but only in cases initiated by Lokpal. In respect of all corruption cases investigated by CBI, State Vigilance Bureaus and State Police, the condition of sanction for prosecution would continue to shield the corrupt. That robbed the government's Lokpal Bill of much of its efficacy in tackling corruption. If corruption was to be tackled effectively, the provision of mandatary sanction for prosecution of corrupt public servants must be removed from the statute book. The Supreme Court's landmark verdict dated 31 January 2012 regarding the provision of sanction for prosecution in corruption cases was an incidental fall out of Subramanium Swamy's petition in respect of the 2G Spectrum Scam. It addressed part of Swamy's complain regarding the delay of 16 months on the part of P.M.'s office in responding to his letter seeking sanction for prosecution of the then Telecom Minister A. Raja on charge of corruption in Spectrum allocation. The government had contended that Swamy, a private citizen, had no right to seek the prosecution of the then Telecom Minister in the matter. Rejecting the government's plea, the Supreme Court upheld the constitutional right of a citizen like Swamy to lodge complaint against public servants regarding corruption and seek sanction for their prosecution from the competent authority. If the sanction is not received within four months, it would be deemed to have been granted. That was kind of an enabling or facilitating verdict.

The substantive verdict of the Supreme Court on the 2G Spectrum Scam itself came on 2nd February 2012. And it was like a bomb shell dropped on the government's handling of the Spectrum allocation issue. Disposing of three relevant petitions on the subject, the Supreme Court pronounced that the entire exercise of allocation of Spectrum licenses by the then Minister A. Raja was arbitrary and illegitimate. Accordingly, the court cancelled a total of 122 2G spectrum licenses granted illicitly by A. Raja, the then Telecom Minister, in 2008. Simultaneously; it directed the three licensee companies Etisalat DB Telecom, Tata Tele Services and Unitech Wireless group, which had sold their shares after obtaining licenses, to pay fines amounting to Rs. Five Corores each. Other such companies namely Loop Telecom, S-Tel, Allianze Infrate and systema Shyam Tele Services were fined Rs. 50 Lakhs each.

Thus a mega scam which had been kept under the carpet by the government since 2008 came to light in 2012, with a bang, thanks to the untiring pursuit of the matter by Subramanium Swamy. Commenting on swamy's stellar role in exposing this super scam, now confirmed by the highest judiciary, the editor of well known satirical magazine "Tughlak', Cho Ramaswamy, observed that he was not only the 'Man of the match' but also the 'Man of the Series'. Being fully satisfied by the Supreme Court's clinical and categorical verdict on the scam, Subramaniam Swamy observed that A. Raja, only a 'small fish' was in jail while 'big fishes' were still out.

The basic fact of the scam is that 2G spectrum licenses were awarded or sold off in 2008 at the same rate as in 2001 even while the market value of 2G Spectrum had increased many fold due to sharp rise in the number of cell phone users. As of now, around 800 million mobile phones are in use in India as against about three to four millions in 2001. In this background, spectrum allocation at throw away rates was nothing short of open loot of country's valuable natural resources. Apart from the gross under valuation of Spectrum prices, the manner in which ground rules were changed in order to help favourite companies to get licenses was not only suspect but patently wrong and illegitimate. In its 85 page judgment, the Supreme Court has observed that in spite of the Finance Secretary's note that the procedure being adopted by A. Raja would be wrong, the Minister went ahead with his arbitrary action in grant of licenses. The fact that some of the licensee companies sold of their equities to other companies at highly infated prices confirmed the fact of gross under valuation in spectrum allocation by the Minister.

The full dimension of the scam in respect of the beneficiaries and government functionaries with whose connivance it happened was under investigation by CBI when Supreme Court pronounced its monumental verdict on it. Leaving no scope for political power-wielders to influence the course of investigation, the appex court authorised the CVC to monitor the course of investigation. Simultaneously, the court directed the CBI to submit progress report of investigation to CVC from time to time and the latter to submit it to the court in sealed cover. That only underlines the magnitude of the scam over which the government had been sleeping for nearly three years.

It also emphasises the importance of higher judiciary in curbing the menace of corruption and facilitating clean governance. In absence of an ombudsman or Lokpal, it is judicial activism which is instrumental in keeping the rapacious power-wielders in check by giving recognition and due weight to Public Interest Litigation (PIL).

It may be recalled that the notorious Bihar Fodder Scam would have remained under the carpet, as the 2G Spectrum Scam had been for three years, but for the intervention of the Patna High Court and the Supreme Court in late 1990's. It was through the route of Public Interest Litigation, now a settled course of action, that the higher judiciary came into the picture and enabled the big scam to be exposed. Higher Judiciary has thus emerged as the great redeemer of the system of governance in the country, as amply demonstrated in the 2G Spectrum and Bihar Fodder Scams.

18

Extent and Magnitude of Corruption in India

It is well known that India is affected by rampant corruption. This has been confirmed by various surveys conducted by reputed international organizations from time to time.

CORRUPTION SURVEYS AND INDICES

An overview of corruption surveys shows that corruption is widespread and entrenched at all levels of the Indian society.

- India ranks 85 from among 180 countries surveyed in *Transparency International's, Corruption Perception Index* (CPI) 2008 with a score of 3.4.
- As per 2007 *World Bank Governance Indicators,* the country performs above average on indicators of government effectives and rule of law, but poorly in terms of regulatory quality and control of corruption.
- *Freedom House* 2008 comes to similar conclusions, noting that government accountability continues to be undermined by close connections between crime and politics and widespread corruption, among other things.
- According to *Global Corruption Barometer* 2007, petty corruption is common practice in India with 25 per cent of the respondents admitting paying bribes to obtain basic services. 90per cent of the respondents believed that corruption would increase in next three years, while 68

per cent perceived government efforts against corruption as ineffective.

- A corruption survey published in 2008 by *Transparency International India* and *Center for Media Studies India* confirms these findings. One-third of Below Poverty Line (BPL) households covered by the survey paid bribe to access one or more of the public services.

- India is also perceived to export corruption outside its borders. As per *Transparency International's* 2008 *Bribe Payer Index,* India ranks 19 from 22 countries. This indicates that Indian firms are perceived by business people as very likely to engage in bribery when doing business abroad.

- An analysis of bribery demands in India conducted by *Trace International* in 2009 shows that in 77 per cent of cases, bribe demands were made for avoiding harm rather gaining an advantage. Of these, more than 51per cent were for the timely delivery of services to which the individual was already entitled, such as clearing customs or getting a telephone connection.

- The *World Bank Enterprise Survey* 2006 revealed that almost 48 per cent of the firms surveyed expected to pay informal payments to public officials to get thing done. Around 26 per cent of the respondents identified corruption as a major constraint for doing business in India. Around 40 per cent of persons reported paying bribes to get an electrical connection and 27 per cent to get a water connection. 52 per cent of the firms reported being expected to give gifts in meetings with tax officials.

- Companies ranked corruption as the fourth most problematic factor in doing business in India according *to World Economic Forum* Global Competitiveness Report-India, 2007-08.

- According to *World Bank* Country Procurement Assessment Report 2003, the average bribe to obtain a public contract is estimated at 15% of the contract's value.

- A Transparency International Report of 2006 on corruption in trucking operations reveals that truck drivers must pay bribes at every stage of their operations to obtain permits, for traffic violations or toll payments. When transporting goods across the country, stoppages by authorities on the pretext of checking documents are frequent. According to the truck drivers, 60 per cent of the checkpoints and stoppages on roads are for extorting money.

THE BLACK MONEY SYNDROME

Corruption in India is, however, not confined to bribery by public servants alone. It has much wider implications linked to the generation and illicit flow of black money in which large sections of the society are involved. The money that is earned and hoarded by dishonest and unfair means and kept in secret to evade taxes is called black-money. It becomes black because no taxes are paid on it. No taxes are paid on it because it is earned by dishonest and unfair means. The massive amount of black money in our country has created a *parallel economy.*

While there are no authentic figures, economists feel that it is in the region of 40 per cent of India's Gross Domestic Product (GDP). Arun Kumar, Professor of Economics, Jawaharlal Nehru University, who has written one of the most authentic books on the subject, *'The Black Economy in India'* (Penguin India, 2002), puts the figure at around 50 per cent of the GDP. According to the latest estimate of Central Statistical Organisation (CSO), the size of the Indian economy is around Rs. 61,64,000 crore. Thus, the size of the black economy, taking it at 40 per cent of GDP, is around Rs. 25,00,000 crore or around $500 billion. If black money is declared by individuals or corporate houses as income, it becomes legal and would be taxed at 30 per cent. If all the estimated black money is declared, it could generate a tax revenue of Rs. 7,50,000 crore for the government! This is more than total tax collection at Rs. 6,41,000 crore for 2009-10. Kumar puts the potential tax revenue figure much higher at around Rs. 10,00,000 crore.

In his book, *Financial Terrorism: Black Money and the*

Indian Elite (Manas, 2010), B.R. Lall, a former Joint Director, CBI and DGP, Haryana, has nicely outlined the process of generation of black money in India. The slush is generated via two routes. First, through the economic activity in the *unaccounted* sector, thereby evading all the taxes, both direct and indirect on this unrecorded GDP by hiding the whole of the economic activity and the consequential incomes generated. Ancillary to this is the income arising out of crime and exploitation that cannot be admitted. Second, by the *evasion* or avoidance of taxes on the incomes generated in the *recorded* sector. In all these cases, taxes are invariably evaded. The incomes generated within the system disappear into the unaccounted stream. The production takes place in the normal course and the goods sell in the market, apparently in the normal course, but the same are not accounted or there is under-accounting. This unaccounted portion is generated either by misappropriating the share of the State by pilfering and misappropriating the resources that belong to the exchequer or by not paying the taxes that may be direct or indirect like sales tax, excise duty and such other taxes. Ultimately, the income tax is also evaded on all such incomes. The goods are freely available in the market without any bills as creation of any record would disturb their applecart. Lall has cited some illustrations by examining the cases of a few areas in order to have a feel of the process of generation of the black money in huge measures.

Gold and Jewellery Industry

Large purchase of gold and diamonds, rather all the costly jewellery is made in cash. The sales tax at two per cent is nominal that no one may like to evade, but since huge amounts of money for purchase of jewellery emanate from black sector, income tax on which has already been evaded, the purchaser cannot give out his real identity and as such prefers transactions in cash. The problem has two aspects. First, the world gold trade is thriving on Indian demand that is largely a function of black money. However, the immediate problem is the Rs. 5 lac crore black money based gold market. The tax evaded on this magnitude of income just 15 per cent (half of standard 30 per cent) would amount to a minimum of Rs. 75,000 crores. This makes it clear why there is so much unrecorded or fake recorded business through cash payment for which much of gold is smuggled into the country which is paid by the black money, here, there and anywhere.

Admission to Professional Colleges

During admissions to professional colleges such as medical, engineering, management, black transactions are frequent. Almost all the private institutes charge the capitation fee in cash for which no receipt is given. For these institutes, this money remains unaccounted and unrecorded. Apart from professional institutions, there is big money involved by way of donations, even in school admissions in most of the private schools, i.e., other than the government schools. However that cannot be assessed in the absence of any reliable data, but since the number of students seeking admission at school level is large, so the financial implications will also be proportionately very high.

Construction Industry

Construction is perhaps the biggest single industry in the country after agriculture. The dark side of this industry came authentically in public view with expositions by Satyendra Dubey. Fired with zeal to serve the nation with a mission, the young IIT graduate spurned cushy jobs and joined NHAI. He protested against the practice of inflating the estimates by 40 per cent at the initial stages and ultimately drawing it from the exchequer by bills, the authenticity of which could not be vouchsafed truthfully. When his struggle in the field was opposed by all, he addressed a letter to the then PM detailing the mechanism and the extent of bungling. When his letter was still circulating the bureaucratic meanders, the information leaked and he was murdered supposedly by the interested groups.

The Builder Phenomenon

It is a well known fact that there is terrible shortage of residential units in the country. Till eighties the individual would purchase a plot and construct a house on his own. A small plot of land was within the reach of the middle and even the lower middle classes. In eighties, the big builders started entering the housing market by acquiring vast tracts of land to be colonized in future.

The prices of colonized land started rising and soared very high in the nineties and in the current decade have skyrocketed. As land prices soared, purchasing even a small plot became difficult and the flat culture ushered in the metropolitan cities and in no time gained popular acceptance. Earlier it had existed in a few big cities like Mumbai, Delhi, etc., but now in view of high prices of land, it has been well received in other smaller cities as well. Considering the costs of the private builder, first his purchase of land is at very economic rates. As the state initiates steps to acquire land in a particular location, the builders enter and purchase the land in the neighbourhood by offering a little higher price. They ascertain the plans in advance through their influence as also through corrupt practices and enter even before the state agencies enter that area. They park their black money or the deposits collected from the applicants and acquire vast chunks of land for being colonized at future dates.

Black Money in SEZ

Special Economic Zone (SEZ) is a good concept as a hub of industrial activity and a facilitator for industrial growth. It leads to the growth of general and industrial infrastructure along with housing, market areas, and educational institutions, all growing together and supporting one another. But unfortunately, SEZs have been drawn into serious controversies involving big scams and sources of generation of black money and concentration of power. Under the garb of developing the industry, huge chunk of land is arranged to be purchased for each SEZ. These lands arranged in bulk lie unused for a number of years. A few years later only, they develop and commence sales at very high price bearing no relation with what they had paid. It has many adverse effects on the economy commencing with the bungling right at the stage of purchase of land.

Tax Evasion

In India, ever since Independence, our business and industry have been at great pains to drive home that tax rates in our country have been very high and that has always been cited as a justification for evasion of taxes. There is no doubt that the tax rates in India at one stage were very high. However, as pointed out by B.R. Lall (in the book cited earlier), the collection of union taxes continued to be one of the lowest in the world at 4.32 per cent of the GDP in 1950-51, of which direct taxes formed only 1.88 per cent. With the rising rates, the amount of taxes collected did go up, but only slightly and remained on a single digit till the year 2003-04. Even in 1973-74 when the marginal rate of individual tax was very high and so were the rates of indirect taxes, the total collection was only 8.18 per cent (of which direct taxes constituted only 2.22 per cent of the GDP). For the first time in 2003-2004, the amount collected as taxes by the Union Government crossed into the double digits and is 10 plus at present as against the world average of 26 percent for the central taxes. The situation in states is no better. Even when all the state taxes all over the country are included, the ratio of total taxes collected to GDP works out to 17.7 per cent in 2008 as against 36 per cent in OECD countries and many other countries all over the world. If our tax rates are higher than other countries why our tax collections fall short in comparison to them as percentage of the GDP? With higher rates, our collections should also be higher, but evasion being general, our collections fall short. Such huge evasion is possible as the elite consider misappropriation of taxes as a perk and a privilege, as pointed by the Gorwala Committee as early as in 1951. The Committee examined the macro aspects from the angle of evasion of taxes. As quoted in the introduction, he brought out clearly how the big people were evading taxes while small men were even unnecessarily being harassed.

Banking Secrecy Laws Abroad

It is the banking secrecy that makes hiding and keeping slush funds possible. As such the Swiss banks and their likes have a very prominent role in facilitating and perpetuating corruption by guaranteeing enjoyment of its fruit through their secrecy. Kickbacks are often credited into accounts abroad to avoid detection. Money duly laundered, may sometimes be brought back to India through normal banking channels, by showing it as gift from some relative or friend, or simply the payment earned through exports. These days laundering centers like Mauritius have sprung up and India is said to receive back its own money in form of

FDI. Even if it is argued that money is flowing back, still the exchequer loses the tax and now has to shell out various concessions on this so-called FDI. The most popular route is through *hawala* channels though corporates often take the easier and more undetectable route of *under-invoicing* exports and *over-invoicing* imports. The select few Indian citizens continue to bleed the nation dry in collusion with global tax havens which have earned the tag of being parasitical. As of now, there is a plethora of ways that the rogue citizens have been employing to get their money deposited illegally in secret accounts abroad.

The process of corruption has been neatly sketched out by B.R. Lall in another book as under:

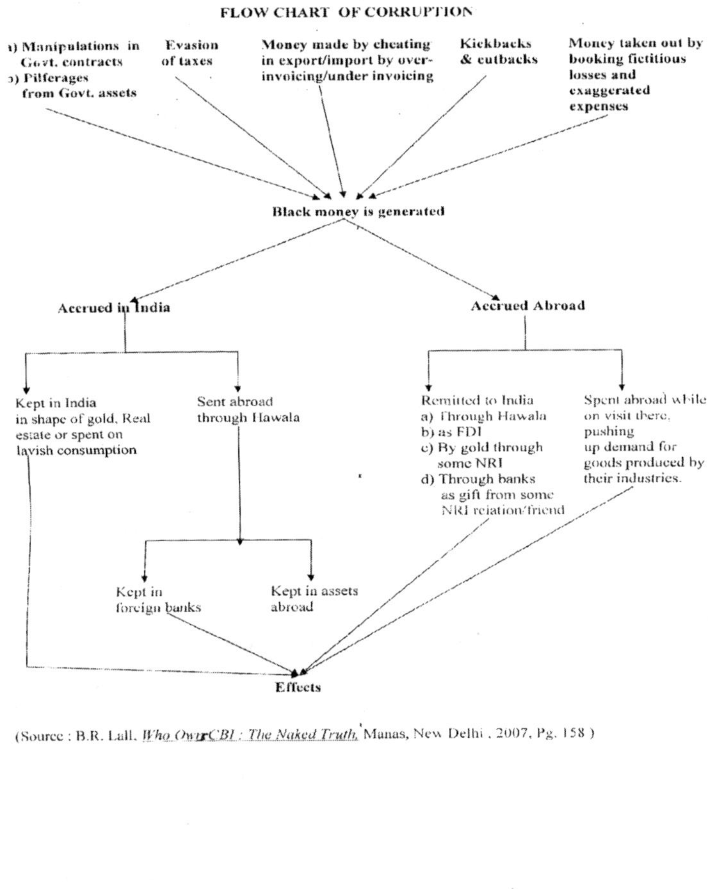

(Source : B.R. Lall, *Who Owns CBI : The Naked Truth,* Manas, New Delhi , 2007, Pg. 158)

BLACK MONEY STASHED IN FOREIGN BANKS

This brings us to another area of darkness in India's corruption scenario-the huge amount of black money deposited by Indian citizens in foreign banks. Indians are the biggest depositors of illegal money in tax havens abroad like Switzerland, Mauritius, Lichtenstein, British Virgin Islands and others.

A *tax haven* has been described as a state or a country or territory where certain taxes are levied at a low rate or not at all while offering due process, good governance and a low corruption rate. Individuals and/or corporate entities can find it attractive to move themselves to areas with reduced or nil taxation levels. This creates a situation of tax competition among governments. Different jurisdictions tend to be havens for different types of taxes, and for different categories of people and/or companies. States that are sovereign or self-governing under international law have theoretically unlimited powers to enact tax laws affecting their territories, unless limited by previous international treaties. *(http://en.wikipedia.org/wiki/tax_haven)*

There are several definitions of tax havens. *The Economist* has tentatively adopted the description by Geoffrey Colin Powell: "What... identifies an area as a tax haven is the existence of a composite tax structure established deliberately to take advantage of, and exploit, a worldwide demand for opportunities to engage in tax avoidance." *The Economist* points out that this definition would still exclude a number of jurisdictions traditionally thought of as tax havens. Similarly, others have suggested that any country which modifies its tax laws to attract foreign capital could be considered a tax haven. According to other definitions, the central feature of a haven is that its laws and other measures can be used to evade or avoid the tax laws or regulations of other jurisdictions.

In its December 2008 report on the use of tax havens by American corporations, the U.S. *Government Accountability Office* was unable to find a satisfactory definition of a tax haven but regarded the following characteristics as indicative of a tax haven:

1. nil or nominal taxes;
2. lack of effective exchange of tax information with foreign tax authorities;
3. lack of transparency in the operation of legislative, legal or administrative provisions;
4. no requirement for a substantive local presence; and
5. self-promotion as an offshore financial center.

The *Organisation for Economic Co-operation and Development* (OECD) identifies three key factors in considering whether a jurisdiction is a tax haven:

1. *Nil or only nominal taxes.* Tax havens impose nil or only nominal taxes (generally or in special circumstances) and offer themselves, or are perceived to offer themselves, as a place to be used by non-residents to escape high taxes in their country of residence.
2. *Protection of personal financial information.* Tax havens typically have laws or administrative practices under which businesses and individuals can benefit from strict rules and other protections against scrutiny by foreign tax authorities. This prevents the transmittance of information about taxpayers who are benefiting from the low tax jurisdiction.
3. *Lack of transparency.* A lack of transparency in the operation of the legislative, legal or administrative provisions is another factor used to identify tax havens. The OECD is concerned that laws should be applied openly and consistently, and that information needed by foreign tax authorities to determine a taxpayer's situation is available. Lack of transparency in one country can make it difficult, if not impossible, for other tax authorities to apply their laws effectively. 'Secret rulings', negotiated tax rates, or other practices that fail to apply the law openly and consistently are examples of a lack of transparency. Limited regulatory supervision or a government's lack of legal access to financial records are contributing factors.

The issue of bringing back this vast capital stocked by corrupt Indian depositors has been popping up from time to time in various forums. Opposition political parties and social activists have been raising their voices urging the government to take effective steps to bring back the funds and expose the looters of the country's wealth. It may be recalled that yoga guru, Ramdev's big movement in mid-2011 launched at Delhi Ramlila ground, which ended with midnight police brutality on his followers, was directed against this drain of India's wealth by corrupt Indians.

Earlier, Subramaniam Swamy, the inveterate campaigner against politicians' corruption, had moved the Supreme Court to ask the government to disclose the names of Indian citizens having secret accounts in Swiss banks. He had been raising the issue time and again and even claimed to have confidential information about some of the political bigwigs of India having secret accounts in Swiss banks. He organised a meeting at Mavlankar Hall, Delhi, in the first week of February, 2012 to declare a war on black money and corruption, which was also attended by Baba Ramdev. On this occasion, he announced the formation of an organization entitled *Action Committee against Corruption in India* comprising many eminent academicians and social activists to carry forward the fight against corruption.

Even as the ding-dong battle of words between government spokespersons and Subramaniam Swamy and others demanding disclosure of the names of foreign bank account holders was going on intermittently, the debate on black money received a boost from an unexpected quarter. On 13 February, 2012, speaking at the inauguration of First Interpol Global Programme on anti-corruption and asset recovery, Amar Pratap Singh, Director, CBI, disclosed: "It is estimated that around 500 billion dollars of illegal money belonging to Indians is deposited in tax havens abroad. Largest depositors in Swiss banks are reported to be Indians." That comes to around a whooping Rs. 24.5 lakh crores of illegal money stashed away by India's corrupt brigade in foreign banks. There had been wide speculation about the quantum of wealth drain by corrupt Indians to tax havens abroad for quite some time. This was confirmed by none other than the Government's own top official who ought to know.

Dwelling upon the legal and procedural hurdles in tracing, confiscation and repatriation of illicit deposits, the CBI Director further observed: "In some of the recent important cases being investigated by the CBI such as 2G, CWG and Madhu Koda, we find that money is taken to Dubai, Singapore, Mauritius, from where it goes to Switzerland and other such tax havens. For criminals, all it involves is setting up a few shell companies and making multi-layered transfers from one account to another in a matter of hours, as there are no boundaries in making banking transactions."

As the super cop in the vanguard of the battle against corruption, A.P. Singh did not mince words when he described corruption as a major governance issue. He went on to elaborate: "Ethics in governance would hold key to good governance in any society. I am prompted to recall a famous verse from the ancient scriptures which says, yatha raja, tatha praja; in other words, if the king is immoral, so be his subjects." *(The Times of India,* Patna, 14, Feb, 2012).

That said it all. What more could a top government official in charge of the existing anti-corruption regime in the country could say on the corruption syndrome. Incidentally, this was the first time that a top government official quantified the estimated wealth drain by corrupt Indians to foreign banks at 24.5 lakh crore (500 billion dollar). That comes to around 50 times the annual allocation for National Rural Employment Guarantee Programme meant for poverty alleviation in rural areas. That speaks volumes about the scale of loot of the country's wealth by the corrupt. And that represents the darkest area of India's transparency status.

A pandora's box has been opened in regard to the estimated amount of black money deposits in foreign banks. Diverse agencies and activists had been flaunting varying estimates of the quantum of this wealth drain. Before India's independence, wealth drain by the British rulers was a common charge and slogan against them in the freedom movement. Ironically, after independence wealth drain to foreign countries by our own corrupt citizens has *surpassed* that by the British. It has been a major hurdle in the path of faster economic growth.

A Report on "*The Drivers and Dynamics of Illicit Financial Flows (IFFs) from India: 1948-2008*," released by *Global Financial Integrity (GFI)*, estimates that tax evasion, crime, and corruption have removed gross illicit assets from India worth US $462 billion. The report also finds that the faster rates of economic growth since economic reform started in 1991 led to a deterioration of income distribution which led to more illicit flows from the country. Moreover, the report finds that the poor state of governance is reflected in a growing underground economy which in turn has fueled more transfers of illicit capital from India. This analysis is cast in terms of a pre- and a post-reform period spanning a total of 61 years since independence.

"This report puts into stark terms the financial cost of tax evasion, corruption, and other illicit financial practices in India," said Global Financial Integrity director Raymond Baker. "It also shows that these illicit outflows contribute to stagnating levels of poverty and an ever widening gap between India's rich and poor."

Primary report findings include:

- From 1948 through 2008, India lost a total of US $213 billion in illicit financial flows (or illegal capital flight). *These illicit financial flows were generally the product of tax evasion, corruption, bribery and kickbacks, and criminal activities.*
- Adjusted Estimates: The present value of *India's total illicit financial flows (IFFs) is at least US $462 billion.* This is based on the short-term U.S. Treasury bill rate as a proxy for the rate of return on assets.
- India's aggregate illicit flows are more than twice the current external debt of US $230 billion.
- Based on the last five years of the study, 2004-2008, India lost assets at a rate of US $19 billion per year.
- Total capital flight out of India represents approximately 16.6 per cent of India's GDP as of year-end 2008. In pre cent value terms, India lost an equivalent of about 36

per cent of its 2008 GDP which represents a staggering loss of capital.

- Some 68 per cent of India's aggregate illicit capital loss occurred after India's economic reforms in 1991, indicating that deregulation and trade liberalisation actually contributed to accelerated the transfer of illicit money abroad.
- *IFF Drivers:* High Net-Worth Individuals (HNWIs) and private companies were found to be the primary drivers of illicit flows out of India's private sector. India's underground economy is also a significant driver of illicit financial flows.
- *IFF Trends:* From 1948 through 2008 the Indian private sector shifted away from deposits into developed country banks and moved more of its money into offshore financial centers (OFCs). The share of OFC deposits increased from 36.4 per cent in 1995 to 54.2 per cent in 2009.

"In this report we clearly demonstrate how India's underground economy is closely tied to illicit financial outflows," said GFI lead economist and report author, Dr. Dev Kar. "The total present value of India's illicit assets held abroad accounts for approximately 72 per cent of India's underground economy. This means that almost three-quarters of the illicit assets comprising India's underground economy—which has been estimated to account for 50 per cent of India's GDP (approximately US $640 billion at the end of 2008)—ends up outside of the country. We also find that there is a statistical correlation between larger volumes of illicit flows and deteriorating income distribution."

The report also makes recommendations for economic reforms and good governance measures and contains comprehensive tables, charts, and other data for detailed analysis of India's illicit financial flows, economic indices, and history of financial reforms.

In a hard-hitting article in *The Hindu,* Feb. 26, 2011, Prof. Arun Kumar (whose book on black economy was cited earlier), has observed that technically, we know how to check the black economy but the problem is political. Is the government finally serious about bringing back the black funds stashed away abroad, variously estimated to be between $ 462 billion and several trillions of dollars? These figures seem credible when one considers the scale of the current scams (tens of billions of dollars) and the case of Hasan Ali where the tax demand runs into billions of dollars. The CD containing names of Indians with bank accounts in the LTG bank which the Indian government accepted in March 2009, a year-and-a-half after it was offered by the German government, has added to the pressure on the government. (Liechtenstein is a small principality of 35,000 people on the German border. The Bank of Liechtenstein was known for its secrecy. Germany won over one of its employees and obtained a pen drive containing information about secret accounts with the bank. The information disclosed the names of not only German citizens, but also from other nations around the world, including India). There are 77 tax havens where illegal funds are stashed away; Switzerland is only the biggest and best known.

According to Prof. Kumar, the government's actions seem to be in direct proportion to the public pressure on it as exposes come in thick and fast. The problem is not new, so what explains the earlier inaction? Consider Bofors or the 2G spectrum case. Initially there has been denial and then minimal action, allowing the culprits' time to escape (as in Hasan Ali's case where the money has disappeared). Rs. 35 lakh crore in black income is generated annually and about 10 per cent of it goes abroad. The capital lost through this route is greater than annual net foreign investment, yet action is minimal. The government pleads that tax havens do not reveal names unless criminality is established and that the Swiss government does not treat tax evasion as a crime. The moot point is why did the Swiss government announce the immediate freezing of Hosni Mubarak's assets without the Egyptian government giving any evidence of criminality? Further, why did UBS agree first to give the names of 250 U.S. citizens and then another 4,500 names to the U.S. tax authorities in 2007-08 without any criminality being individually established? In the Hasan Ali case, the Swiss government has said that it has not been given the information required. Similarly, in Ottavio Quattrocchi's case, the Indian government has twice lost in foreign courts because the case has not been properly established. In 1992, Madhavsinh Solanki, then Minister of External Affairs, passed on a chit to a Swiss Minister apparently to slow down the Bofors case but the Narasimha Rao government quietly buried the embarrassment by accepting his resignation. The few cases of corruption initiated against the high and mighty are apparently spoilt or not pursued. Given this history, will there be seriousness this time or will the government wait out the storm? In the last 60 years, dozens of committees have studied various aspects of the black economy and given thousands of suggestions. Hundreds of these suggestions have been implemented but the size of the black economy has grown exponentially. The Wanchoo Committee report bulges with suggestions. Since 1971, when the highest tax rate was 97.5 per cent, tax rates have fallen but the black economy has grown from 7 per cent to 50 per cent of GDP. Controls and regulations have been drastically eliminated after 1991 but the size of black economy continues to rise. The causes of black income generation lie elsewhere. The recent rise in corporate tax collection is a reflection of rising disparity and not better compliance. Plugging loopholes has only made the laws more complex, as in the case of taxation. The ingenuity of the corrupt thwarts the enforcement agencies by either devising newer ways of circumventing the law or simply bribing the officials. In India, laws on paper and in practice differ because of the *'triad'* of the corrupt business class, the political class, and the executive. In brief, technically we know what needs to be done to check the black economy — but the problem is political. The top echelons of the leadership are the prime drivers of the black economy. They do not wish to forgo the massive illegal profits they generate. So how can the political will be generated? A voluntary disclosure scheme to bring back black savings stashed away abroad for 'development' is being considered. Wasn't the Mauritius route created to allow round tripping of funds? It has accelerated black income generation by facilitating it. A National Security Adviser alerted the nation to terror funds entering the stock markets to destabilise the financial markets. The Wanchoo Committee argued that this kind of scheme makes honest people dishonest. A report of the Comptroller and Auditor General of India on the 1997 voluntary disclosure scheme pointed out that the same people who declared their black incomes earlier took advantage of the 1997 scheme — becoming habitual tax offenders.

Some argue that elections underlie black income generation and corruption. Presently, when a Lok Sabha constituency sees the expenditure of crores of rupees per serious candidate, state funding will make little difference. At best, it can be to the tune of the allowed election expenditure of Rs. 25 lakh — just a few per cent of the actual expenditure by most candidates. Further, according to Prof. Kumar, what is spent on the national elections officially and unofficially is not even one per cent of GDP for that year; so this cannot be the cause of black incomes. It is the black economy that works to subvert the elections. Genuine democracy would not be expensive. Today, we have formal democracy with weak content. In this background, it is clear that the government's actions against corruption will be in proportion to the public outrage and that too the minimum necessary. It is likely that there will be pretence while the real culprits go scot-free. Setting up a committee is to buy time and to stall questions on the subject since the government can claim it is waiting for the report. Later, it can buy time by pretending to look into the recommendations or bury an inconvenient report (like the Vora Committee report). In the liberalised environment, those with black money stashed away abroad can turn into non-residents overnight and escape prosecution in India. This is perhaps the reason the Indian government is unable to proceed against the entities named in the Liechtenstein disc. For the rest, little money may be left in their accounts, given the inordinate delays. Taxation treaties being entered into by the government with other governments are all about legal incomes traceable to known individuals. But black incomes are typically parked via shell companies and in benami accounts. What is needed is serious investigation and prosecution in the country that will also expose the money siphoned off abroad. Intelligence agencies can provide the leadership with information through tapping and so on, which can be mined instead of being used for political blackmail. The prosecution agencies deliberately spoil cases for political reasons. If prosecution is not possible in India, how can the case be made in foreign lands for booking the culprits? In brief, as Prof. Kumar puts it, the policy pronouncements are delaying and diversionary tactics to allow those generating black incomes to escape via shell companies and benami accounts.

(*http://www. hindu. com/2011/02/26/stories/2011022665791400. htm,* accessed on March 27, 2012).

This, in the background of visible poverty of the common masses, presents a grotesque picture of India's socio-economic development.

19

Lokpal as an Agent of Good Governance

In the ultimate analysis, corruption is an issue or a problem of governance. Widespread corruption among government functionaries at various levels is a major challenge to governance. It not only distorts the delivery mechanism of huge investment in the social sector to improve the lot of the common man (like the National Rural Employment Guarantee Programme) but also puts a question work on the system of governance itself.

Basically, it is a matter of ethics in governance. If ethics is sidelined or ignored, governance becomes susceptible or vulnerable to the virus of corruption. As the scale of wealth creation in the country is accelerated, so does the scale of corruption in absence of ethical norms and standards steering the ship of the nation. This is what seems to have happened in India. With the GDP growth rate pegged at around 03 per cent per annum since independence for a major part of the 20th century, the scope of wealth grabbing by the corrupt was rather limited. That partly accounts for relatively corruption free governance in the Nehru era, as mentioned earlier in Chapter 8; apart of course from the high moral standards maintained by the generation of freedom fighters who held the reigns of governance during that period.

The zinx of sluggish GDP growth rate was eventually broken by adoption of bold economic liberalisation policy by successive governments beginning the last decade of the 20th century. That brought about a quantum jump in India's economic development from a measly three per cent to around 7-8 per cent per annum in the first decade of the 21st century. While it made India one of the fastest developing countries of the world, it also made it vulnerable to large scale corruption, both governmental and corporate. As the kitty of wealth grows big, the scope for grabbing as much of it as possible by the greedy and the corrupt increases accordingly. The unwelcome spurt in corruption in the first decade of the 21st century was an incidental fall-out of the welcome spurt in India's GDP growth rate during this period. In other words, there seems to be a direct correlation between economic development and incidence of corruption in the country.

That is not to decry fast economic development as such or to plead for sacrificing it in order to minimise the incidence of corruption. Far from it.

India's emergence from a stagnant economic status to a fast growing economic entity is a remarkable success story of our times. It is another matter that the benefit of this economic boom has not percolated so as to make a dent in the over all poverty situation of the country. The so-called trickle down effect of the increasing prosperity of the rich resulting from faster economic development has not touched or reached down to the poor standing at the lowest rung of the ladder. This has widened the gap between the rich and the poor, thus increasing the degree of inequality in society without significantly contributing to poverty alleviation in the country. But that is part of another story which is beyond the scope of this book.

In the above back ground of mounting corruption coinciding with fast economic development, a holistic approach is needed to counter it through good governance. For this a new structure of governance is needed to address the problem through a slew of corrective legislative enactments. These should include, interalia, tougher laws to deal with money laundering, tax evasion, foreign exchange violations, illicit money transfers, etc., and electoral reforms to check the flow of black money in elections and, more importantly, prevent the entry of criminal and corrupt elements in legislative bodies. Electoral reforms have been dealt with at some length in Chapter 15. The other important pillar of governance is Comptroller and Auditor General (CAG) who should be provided with more power to scrutinize the financial transactions of government departments and public sector undertakings. The stellar role of the incumbent CAG in exposing the 26 mega scam has already been dealt with in Chapter 17. Both Chief Election Commissioner and CAG are existing constitutional entities that need to be strengthened.

It is in this context that creation of the institution of Lokpal has to be viewed as an agent of good governance. That in fact was the idea behind the creation of the institution of Ombudsman in Sweden on which the concept of Lokpal is based. The institution of ombudsman was started to oversee the functioning of government officials as a watchdog to keep them on straight path. It evolved in most countries of the world as kind of a correctional mechanism to check malpractices, inefficiencies and improper governmental activities at the cost of citizens. In other words, the institution of ombudsman was conceived and established as an agent of good governance by way of course correction of erring government functionaries. That is the model on which the concept of Lokpal is patterned. It is nobody's case that a Lokpal alone will be a panacea for all the ills of corruption. But a firm and determined beginning has to be made in this direction to send a clear signal to the corrupt persons that they cannot get away with impunity.

In fact, India's first Prime Minister Jawahar Lal Nehru had first talked about it briefly as early as in 1963. Speaking at the AICC meeting at Jaipur on 3rd November 1963, Nehru observed that the ombudsman system fascinated him but he felt that in a big country like India, the introduction of such a system was beset with difficulties. Thus while admiring the idea of a watchdog body like ombudsman, he just fell short of pushing it further. That was understandable in the context of his time which was relatively free from the menace of corruption and misgovernance.

Later, the aborted Lokpal Bill of 1977 had defined "misconduct" to include, besides corruption, failure to act in any case otherwise than in accordance with the norms of integrity and conduct which ought to be followed by the class of public men to which the concerned Minister belonged. That clearly brought out the basic objective of Lokpal as promoting good governance by checking "misconduct" of public men. It is another matter that the JPC (Joint Parliamentary Committee) considered the definition of "misconduct" incorporated in the Bill to be "too wide and therefore likely to be amenable to different interpretations". In any case, this bill was aborted when the Janata dispensation came to an end.

The current debate is focused on the issue of corruption and the role of Lokpal as an anti-corruption institution par excellence. But corruption is just a part of governance deficiency like, for instance, inefficiency and maladministration, which are addressed by ombudsman in other countries. In the present day Indian context, corruption of public men and government functionaries at all levels appears to have become the most important component of governance deficiency which the institution of Lokpal is supposed to address.

Accordingly, it would be relevant now to assess how far Lokpal, as envisaged by Government and Anna's Jan Jokpal can prove equal to the task. The first thing that strikes one is the unwieldy size of Lokpal. The Jan Lokpal proposed by Anna's team is too big and so is the government's. While Jan Lokpal is slated to have 10 members besides the Chairman, the government's Lokpal would have 8 members besides the Chairman. Both are too top-heavy and unwieldy to be functional. Both have failed to recognize that Lokpal is neither a legislative nor a judicial organ. It is supposed to be only a watchdog agency meant for policing the government to check it form going stray. As the saying goes, too many cooks spoil the broth. Other watchdog institutions like the CAG and even the Election Commission have proved their worth without being large in size and unwildy A functional Lokpal should ideally have two or three members besides the Chairperson. For, the limited job of Lokpal is to investigate or get investigated complaints of corruption against public servants and put them for trial before a court of law for judiciary to take over. It should not assume the role of judiciary to give the final verdict.

The second deficiency in the government Lokpal is the absence of any effective investigating agency at its disposal. This can be remedied by placing the anti-corruption wing of the CBI squarely under Lokpal. This would also adequately meet the repeated demand for placing the CBI under the control of an independent agency to prevent its use or misuse by the government in power for partisan interest.

With the installation of Lokpal, the Central Vigilance Commission, as constituted now, would become redundant. It is a purely advisory body with neither an investigation agency of its own nor power to enforce its advice given to central government departments and public sector undertakings concerned. Its stipulated function of reviewing the progress of investigation in cases of corruption by the CBI would become infructuous with merger of CBI in Lokpal.

The general supervisory role assigned to the CVC in matters relating to corruption would come within the purview of Lokpal. It would be appropriate to abolish the CVC and merge its existing staff into the Lokpal. Such a Lokpal, armed with a professional investigating agency like CBI, and having the supervisory jurisdiction of the CVC would be an eminently suitable institution to stem the tide of growing corruption and thereby come up as an agent of good governance.

20

The Unending Lokpal Debate

The Lokpal story, which began around 44 years ago when the first Lokpal Bill was introduced in Parliament in 1968, would not come to an end even after dust settles over Anna's Movement. It would continue to stimulate debates and discussions, arguments and counter arguments in political, legal and intellectual circles for quite sometime. The unending debate over the issue of Lokpal, heating up and cooling down intermittently, has continued for well over 40 years in some form or other. Like the unstoppable stream of corruption scandals, more about which in the next chapter.

It is not generally known that Lokpal Bill also figured in J.P's anti-corruption movement of mid 1970's alongwith such other issues like right to recall and other electoral reforms. Evidently, J.P. had interacted with a wide range of people and cross section of society like lawyers, academicians and activists and scrutinised the Lokpal Bill introduced in Parliament in 1971. He had given a thought to the issue and observed. "Let me not create the impression that the appointment of a Lokpal and Lokayuktas will in itself cure the disease of corruption so rampant among Ministers and civil servants. This is not the place to go into the question, but if the Lokpal Bill and the Maharashtra Lokayukta Act, which is claimed to be patterned after the former were carefully scrutinised, it would be discovered that the action of these vital officers is severely limited and hemmed in by restrictive provisions."

What J.P. said in early 1970's about the Lokpal Bill then on offer was more or less applicable to the official Lokpall Bill on offer in 2012. That would go to show how minimal or little progress was made in enactment of an effective Lokpal Bill in course of the last 40 years. What Anna's anti-corruption movement achieved was to bring it out of the cupboard and put it on the top of the nation's agenda. That in itself was an achievement of sorts for which Anna's team could pat its back.

But that was not going to be the end of the story. For Anna's team has adopted a maximalist position to push forward their own version of Lokpal Bill, that is, the Jan Lokpal Bill, and carry on with their movement for its acceptance by the political class. The Lokpal as envisaged in Anna's scheme would function like the executive in regard to investigation and prosecution and as judiciary in imposing penalties and other modes of punishment to delinquent public servants. It would have powers to investigate and prosecute all 'public servants', which by definition, would include the Prime Minister, other Ministers, Member of Parliament, Judges down to clerks at the lowest level, a tall order by all means.

Another problem with Anna's Jan Lokpal Bill is the cumbersome process of selection of the Lokpal envisaged in it. The selection process laid down in Anna's bill is so complicated that it would be difficult to constitute the Lokpal and put it in place within a reasonable time frame. For instance, before the selection committee takes up the task of selection of chairperson and members of Lokpal an unwieldy search committee would have to send a list of persons considered suitable for appointment as members of Lokpal. The list itself would contain names three times more than the number of persons to be appointed. And before the list is sent for consideration of the selection committee, the names of short listed persons would have to be put on a public website to enable people to send their comments about the so short listed nominees. This would be a repeat exercise because even before the short list is prepared by the search committee, the names of the nominees would have been put on a website for inviting comments from the public about the suitability or otherwise of the nominees.

Even with such a baggage of conditionalities in the selection process, the Anna's team is determined to continue their movement for adoption of their Jan Lokpal Bill. That would mean that the protracted Lokpal debate was slated to continue without coming to a conclusion in the short term. In fact, the over-ambition of Anna's team to create an ombudsman covering the whole country and all aspects of governance at one stroke through a single legislation would in itself be a stumbling block in setting up of Lokpal. Until then, the debeat would continue.

And even if the political stake holders-ruling and opposition parties-manage to create an agreed institution of Lokpal the debate would not stop. For all the arguments and counter arguments for and against different versions of Lokpal indulged in by the stake holders in course of the marathon debate would come into full play once the institution came into being. The foremost among these would be the apprehension of Lokpal emerging as a "monstrous leviathan" or a parallel center of power over-shadowing the democratically elected wielders of power. It was an imaginary apprehension, as discussed in chapter 16 or at best a diversionary plank put forward by those opposed to the installation of an effective ombudsman for obvious reasons. But it would continue to be debated in the post-Lokpal regime, if an when it materialised, as it was in pre-Lokpal period.

In reality, a meaningful Lokpal was only meant to keep an eye on and check corruption from the highest to the grass root level affecting the common man. Nothing more, nothing less.

For, in actual practice, the very existence of Lokpal would keep the corrupt and would-be corrupt in check. Almost like the fear of God that keeps the sinners and would-be sinners in some sort of a check.

Throughout the long debate, it was nobody's case that once installed Lokpal would be a panacea for ridding the country of the hydra-headed monster of corruption. In a well functioning democratic society, it is for the common people to keep a vigilant eye on the practice of corruption by government functionaries and check it. For the common people, or a vast majority of them, are not the practicioners of corruption but victims of it. They are the beneficiaries of the delivery system of economic benefits meant for them through schemes like National Rural Employment Guarantee Programme, National Rural Health Mission. Indira Gandhi Awas Yojna etc. The delivery system has become malfunctional due to prevailing corruption on the part of middle level executives both bureaucratic and political-at the cost of the common people. To the extent that Lokpal or fear of Lokpal was able to rid the delivery mechanism of corruption by reigning in the rapacious government functionaries, the great Lokpal movement would have served its purpose.

21

'Coalgate' or Coal Block Allocations Scam

The UPA government under its famously 'honest' Prime Minister has, paradoxically enough, came to be associated with one major scam after another in a series as no other government had been before. The latest in the series is the Coal Block allocation scam which has come to be known as "Coalgate" after the ill famed "Water gate" scandal that cost the incumbent American President Nixon his Presidency in 1970's.

It relates to free allocation of millions of metric tons of coal blocks to private commercial entities by the Central Government between 2004 and 2009. The scam came to light when the Comptroller and Auditor General (CAG) submitted his report entitled 'Performance Audit of Coal Block Allocations' in 2012 castigating the government for allotting coal block to private companies without competitive bidding. This results in 'undue profits' to private companies and estimated notional loss to government exchequer.

It may be noted that the Coal Mines (Nationalisation) Act of 1973, as amended in 1976, prohibited all persons other than the central government and a government company managed and controlled by the central government to operate coal mines. Thus, all private mining in any form in respect of coal was expressly prohibited. The nationalisation of coal industry gave birth to a giant Government company called Coal India Limited (CIL) which alone was authorized to carry on mining of all coal deposits in the country.

With the advent of the era of economic liberalisation, the prohibition of mining coal by non-government agencies, that is, private companies was partially lifted in 1993 with the passing of Coal Mines (Nationalisation) Amendment Act in that year. Accordingly, the central government or the government company, that is the C.I.L. could authorise a private party to mine coal if reserves of coal are located in isolated small pockets or are not sufficient in quantum for scientific and economic mining operation. This 1993 Amendment of the Nationalisation Act opened the floodgate for successive governments to allot coal blocks arbitrarily to private parties.

This provision for allotment of coal block to private parties on some pretext or the other was a deviation from the spirit of nationalisation of coal industry and went against the long term interest of the country. The very purpose of nationalisation was to prevent reckless extraction of coal for commercial use by private companies coming on since the colonial times. This had wrecked havoc with the coal deposits beneath the earth resulting in huge loss of this valuable national asset. The most glaring example of destruction of coal was the raging fire in coal deposits underneath Jharia township in Jharkhand. This has already resulted in loss of millions of tones of precious coal underneath the earth and the fire is still to be fully extinguished. It was primarily for checking this kind of destructive mining by private parties that coal industry was nationalised and any deviation from it has to be viewed with suspicion. Infact, large scale allocation of coal blocks to private companies for Commercial exploitation defeats the very purpose of nationalisation of coal industry, it amounts to frittering away of this precious national asset to enable selected parties to reap undue profits.

Precious asset indeed is coal reserve for India because it is a fossil fuel which is exhaustible. It is not like air or water which are inexhaustible and can be used by humans for ages. Even drinking water is now being considered as a valuable natural resource with bulging human population necessitating adequate conservation. Coal is a different proposition altogether because its stock underneath the earth in India is limited and exhaustible.

The urgency of conservation of our precious coal deposits and rationalisation of its utilisation is underlined by the key position of coal in Indian economy. For production of steel, high quality of coking coal is required which is already scarce in India. And the rest of steam coal accessible is the most important industrial fuel to keep the wheels of production moving. A host of large scale industries like cement, aluminum, etc., and medium and small scale business units engaged in production of secondary goods like agricultural tools require steam coal to keep going and above all, coal is the main and single most important source of electrical energy in India. Thermal power is the largest energy source in India which is based entirely on coal. As such, coal is the most valuable natural asset of India like the oil deposits of Arab countries. It is not only black gold, as is often described, but black diamond. And its quantum is unfortunately limited and exhaustible.

It is in this background that the CAG's report on free allocation of coal blocks to private companies has to be viewed. If the government had to allot coal blocks to private companies for commercial exploitation, which in itself was a suspect proposition open to corruption, it was duty bound to realise its price based on the profits that the allotee companies were calculated to make. Failure to realise the legitimate price of coal blocks to a large number of private companies was thus a grave financial irregularity which has been adversely commented upon in the CAG's report. CAG has affirmed that the government had given "undue benefits" to the extent of around Rs. 1.8 lakh crores to commercial entities, most of them being private companies, through free allocation of coal blocks.

As indicated in CAG's report, a meeting headed by the Prime Minister on 14 Oct. 2004 had decided that all future allocation of coal blocks would be through competitive bidding so that genuinely efficient companies could secure allotment and government could get its due share of the profits accruing to the allotee private companies. Accordingly, a cut off date of 28 June 2004 was also fixed at this meeting after which all applications for coal blocks were to be dealt with through competitive bidding route.

And yet, the coal department continued the practice of allotting coal blocks to private companies by a so-called screening committee arbitrarily instead of competitive bidding. Thus, 61 coal blocks were allotted to private companies without competitive bidding in 2006 alone. Not only that, around 3000 metric tons of coal blocks were allocated to two private companies, a Tata group joint venture and a Jindal group unit on 27 february 2009, about a month before the Lok Sabha election that year. That tells its own story. The close proximity of these last minute coal block allocations to 2009 Lok Sabha elections lends credibility to opposition charge that illicit money was collected by the ruling party to finance its election campaign through these allocations.

In course of hearing on a PIL filed by an advocate, the Supreme Court observed "This is not distribution of state properties in a small way. It is mines of largesse, not even tons of largesse. By the way, is it a mere coincidence that so many politicians, their relatives or supporters were benefitted in the 194 coal block allotments?" (Quoted in '*The Times of India*'. Patna edition dated 15 September 2012) That speaks volumes about the scale and dimensions of the coal blocks allocation scam.

A telling example of how coal blocks were allocated violating all norms and without an iota of justification is the case of allocation of Rajhara North Coal Block. This coal block was a part of coal deposits reserved for the government company Coal India Limited (CIL) and very much mineable by it. In fact, the CIL had requested the coal ministry in January 2008 not to de-reserve the Rajhara North Coal block. And yet, this coal block was taken away from C.I.L and handed over to a private company Vini Iron and Steel Udyog Limited in November 2008. It may be noted that this Vini company was one of the 18 fake companies set up by the disgraced Jharkhand Ex-CM Madhu Koda accused in Rs. 4000 crore Koda scam.

The real issue that has emerged from the CAG report is not the estimated loss to the exchequer but the lack of transparency and arbitrariness in coal block allocations by the government. By avoiding the route of competitive bidding, the government opened the floodgate of corruption in coal block allocations. The so-called 'screening committee which processed the allocations and chose the allotees virtually turned out to be "crony" committee which picked and chose favourite private companies arbitrarily providing scope for free play ot corruption in the entire process. That is the most sinister aspect of the coal block allotment scam.

A joke doing the rounds in coal India circles (where this writer had worked as Chief of Vigilance for over four years during 1979-1983) went as follows. Anyone who dealt with or handled coal lined his pocket and blackened his face. How true! As regards the space for corruption in the manner in which coal blocks were allotted between 2004 and 2009, the CAG report has touched only the tip of the iceberg.

The CAG report, in accordance with its constitutional mandate, was confined to examining and assessing the financial irregularities resulting in loss of government revenue and undue benefits to private parties. But the key issue in the entire coal block allocation exercise is the scope for and magnitude of corruption involved in it. This is confirmed by the slew of cases registered against several coal block allotees by the CBI. Forced by the political storm which consumed the entire monsoon session of Parliament in 2012, the government went about reviewing the allocations through an Inter Ministerial Group (the process was continuing at the time of writing). An interesting case that came to light related to Nagpur based Grace Industries Ltd. which had been allotted a coal block. Within a year of the allocation, two directors of the company sold their stakes in the company to another party at a profit of Rs. 20 crore. That would show the wide open space for corruption provided by the practice of coal block allotments by a crony committee.

But first, why go about allocating scarce coal blocks to private parties at all? For proper, well planned and scientific mining of coal in the country, the giant government company Coal India Limited (C.I.L.). with its subsidiaries B.C.C.L, ECL, CCL, W.C.L., etc. is the fittest agency. It may be noted that, as mentioned earlier, the 1993 Amendment of Coal Mines (Nationalisation) Act permitted the government to authorise a private party to mine coal *only if coal reserves were located in isolated small pockets where scientific and economic mining operation by the government company was not possible*. Taking advantage of this enabling provision, government went about allocating coal blocks indiscriminately to a large number of private parties opening the flood gates of corruption in the process.

How the enabling provision of 1993 amendment was abused by the government is illustrated by the case of allotment of Rajhara North Coal Block to a tainted private company in November 2008, as disussed earlier in this chapter. According to an opposition MP, who acted as the whistle blower in the 'coalgate', around 400 skilled CIL employees were declared redundant after the government de-reserved the Rajhara North Block and gifted it to the tainted private company. It is learnt that a large number of workers lost their jobs after similar coal blocks were taken away from the CIL and given to private companies. This reckless gift of largesse to private parties at the expense of CIL and its work force can be explained only by the free play of corruption on the part of government functionaries concerned, both political and bureaucratic. That is the crux of the coal block allocation scam.

Much was being made about by the government trumpeteers about the supremecourt's generic opinion in response to a Presidential reference that auction or competitive bidding could not be the only valid mode of allocation of natural resources by the government. But at the same time, Justice J.S. Khehar, a member of the constitution Bench that answered the presidential reference, said in a separate opinion about coal block allocations that law permited such allocations only through auction and no other way. Referring to the Mines and Minerals (Development and Regulation) Act, Justice Khehar observed: "For the grant of mining lease in respect of an area, containing coal, the provision leaves no room for any doubt that selection would be made through auction by competitive bidding. No process other than auction can therefore be adopted for the grant of coal mining lease." (Quoted in '*The Times of India*' Patna edition dated 28 September 2012).

In the entire debate over the mode of allocation of coal blocks to private parties, the basic concern about preservation of this precious and limited natural resource for future generations has been lost sight of. For if the limited coal reserves beneath our earth are squandered and frittered away for private profit, or may be short term economic benefits, no coal would be left for the posterity to live upon.

On the visibly great prosperity of Arab countries based on their oil deposits, a wig jokingly commented that after their oil deposits are exhausted, the Arab people would restart moving on the back of camels. Even if that happens, for the sake of argument, it would not be so for around another four hundred years or so. On the other hand, there is real possibility of India's coal deposits being exhausted in a hundred years or so. It would be nightmarish to visualise the gave economic scenario if and when India's coal deposits are exhausted. That adds an ominous dimension to the coal block allocations scam.

22

Anna's Movement at the Cross Road

After over a year of retenless drive, propelled by off again and on again Anshan (Fasting) by Anna's team, Anna's movement had reached a cross road.With the government determined not to pay heed to Anna's fast beginning 29 July 2012 and that of his team members Arvind Kejriwal. Manish Sisodia and Gopal Rai earlier, the stalemate continued- That left Anna's team with only two options, One, to continue with Lokpal centric movement with the only means available-prolonged fasting to rouse the conscience of the nation and push forward the government to bring up a meaningful institution of Lokpal. But with the callous indifference of the establishment towards the ethical dimensions of Anna's crusade, resulting in diminishing efficacy of fasting for a noble cause, this option had a bleak prospect. Two, to be more proactive and go overtly political in pursuit of their sacred mission. Anna's team opted for the second course.

This was well summed up by Manish Sisodia at the time of breaking his 'anshan' (fasting) thus: "We are left with just two options. Either we fast for years which will have little impact on the government. But look at Irom Sharmila, has it made a difference? Or we start a political revolution." (Quoted in '*The Times of India*', Patna edition, 4th August 2012) General (Retired) V.K. Singh, ex-Army Chief, who offered a glass of juice to Anna to break his fast at Jantar Mantar on 4th August 2012, took a wide swipe at the government. He observed: "It is an absolute break down of democracy. There is rampant corruption, our GDP is going down, and inflation is so high that the common man is pushed to the edge. We are left with no direction."

Arvind Kejriwal, the most visible and vocal member of Anna's team was more articulate in defining the political path and direction of Anna's movement. He thundered: "We will uproot the current corrupt government. Till now we have been only requesting the government to implement the Jan Lok Pal Bill but now it is a larger movement. *We have to throw them out of power.*" (Quoted in 'The Times of India', Patna edition. 4th August 2012).

That said it all Anna Hazare excused himself personally from joining any political party, but declared that he would move around the country to awaken the people and urge them to bring about a change and rally behind a political alternative. That set the stage for Anna's over a year long high voltage anti-corruption crusade, with high moral over tones, turning into a full fledged political outfit.

There were many dissenting voices among the movement supporters against the decision to enter politics. Medha Patkar and Santosh Hegde were prominent among the dissenters. Medha Patkar made a pertinent comment that when well-meaning people with noble intentions join politics, either they don't last long or they don't achieve much. That was a word of caution which political party enthusiasts in Anna's team could ill afford to ignore. For, politics is a different ball game altogether, in which "India Against Corruption' enthusiasts are not adept. True, idealism is the driving force behind genuine politics, but real politics is much more than idealism.

Medha Patkar's significant comment on Anna's team going political is corroborated by history of our early post-independence years. That relates to the story of the rise and fall of the great Socialist party of India in the immediate post independence years. It continued to function as a wing of the Indian National Congress in pre-independence period ever since its advent in 1930's But soon after independence in 1947 the Indian National Congress, which had as a broad platform for freedom fighters of all hues, turned into an exclusive political party with a defined constitution of its own. The Congress party as such had no place for an identifiable political group with a distinct policy and programme of its own. This resulted in the exit of the socialists from the parent Congress Party and formation of the Socialist Party of India on the lines of the Communist Party of India.

All the young idealists led by Jay Prakash Narain and Ram Manohar Lohia formed the once glamorous Socialist Party of India armed with the attractive ideology of Socialism. Much like the activists of Anna's movement, they aspired to challenge the old guard of the original Indian National Congress and occupy the center stage of India's nascent democracy. With this end in view, they passed a resolution piloted by Lohia in their plenary session at Patna in the spring of 1949 converting the cadre-based socialist party into a mass party. Thus was launched a rejuvenated Socialist Party as a hopefully viable alternative to the old Congress Party which had taken over the mantle from the British colonial regime.

And the leading lights of the socialist party represented a galaxy of luminaries who appeared to be the future of India. They included giants like Acharya Narendra Deo. Jay Prakash Narain, Ram Manohar Lohia, Achyut Patwardhan, Aruna Asaf Ali, Yusuf Meher Ali and Madhu Limaye. With such illustrious personalities in the lead, the Socialist Party challenged the Congress Party in the first general election of independent India in 1952. But what happened? The old Congress Party swept the poll and the Socialists were nearly wiped out. J.P.'s disenchantment with electoral politics was complete. So much so that he quit politics, or electoral politics to be precise, and joined Vinoba Bhave's Bhoodan movement in June 1954.

That was the background of Medha Patkar's cautionary comment on the prospect of jumping into electoral politics. On 06 August 2012, Anna himself disbanded what came to be branded as 'Team Anna' and returned to his home village. Ralegan Siddhi. He would continue to keep up the pressure and momentum for setting up a strong Lokpal in his own way. If the government did not install a strong watch dog to curb corruption Anna would work to elect good people in 2014 Lok Sabha elections to bring it up. But he did not hide his concern about the risks involved in his movement taking a political turn. He posed pertinent questions as to how would the members of the proposed political party be selected, where would the money for running the party come from, how would the candidates for election be selected and so on.

Anna's aversion to the idea of forming or joining a political party grew by the day as he sat in Ralegan Siddhi mulling over the issue. In his firm "no" to his movement turning into a political outfit, Anna was supported by such mature members of his erstwhile team like Santosh Hegde and Kiran Bedi. The doubt and debate over the issue among the movement supporters continued until 19 September 2012 when the entire group met at Delhi for a threadbare discussion. After a marathon in-house debate, Anna finally announced his firm decision not to form or join a political party and parting of the way from Arvind Kejriwal and his group which opted for a political course. He proclaimed that his great movement had split.

It was with a tinge of sadness that Anna announced his parting of the way from Kejriwal & Co. He regretted that his erstwhile famous team, which the government could not break, got split due to internal differences. He, however, affirmed that though they had chosen to go along different routes their destination was the same-a corruption free society. As an earthy grass root level activist who had experienced the ground level political reality, Anna had unconcealed contempt for the practice of politics in the country. He gave vent to it when he visited Delhi for the second time on 30 September 2012 and on return to his sanctuary at Ralegan Siddhi. to chalk out the next course of action on his non-political or a political anti-corruption crusade. He minced no words when he said that politics was "full of dirt" while his anti-corruption agitation was "sacred". With Arvind Kejriwal determined to form a political party, and Anna equally determined not to connect with it, the split in Anna's once big movement was complete.

23

Kejriwal's New Avatar as a Political Leader

With Anna shutting the opening to the political route loud and clear on 30 September 2012, the stage was set for Kejriwal & Co. to plunge into the uncharted ocean of politics. They did it in style on 2nd October 2012 when Arvind Kejriwal addressed a 1000 strong gathering of his supporters at the Constitution Club Delhi announcing the launching of his political party. The vision document of the party promised free health care and education for all, prices of essential commodities to be fixed by the common man, no land acquisition without people's concent, special policies for the benefit of SC/ST/OBC's and minorities and of course Jan Lokpal within ten days of being elected. Addressing to Anna's concern about the corrupting influence of politics. Kejriwal cited the example of political leaders like Lal Bahadur Shastri. Ram Manohar Lohia, B.R. Ambedkar and Jyoti Basu arguing that these leaders had entered electoral politics without compromising on their ideals.

The vision document of the party contained all the goodies like curbing corruption, containing inflation, bringing back black money, ensuring fair prices for farm products and electoral reforms like right to reject and right to recall. Proclaiming that it would be a political party with a difference, the group released a protocol for the party candidates banning them from enjoying the perks and frills of office like travelling in vehicles with redlights, keeping a bunch of security guards as a status symbol and living in official houses. If elected, no M.P. or MLA of this party would enjoy the pleasure of occupying big bungalows. They would have to live in modest houses like the common man.

Old timers recalled that Kejriwal's parting of the way from Anna Hazare was somewhat similar to what happened when Netaji Subhas Chandra Bose broke away from Mahatma Gandhi to form his Forward Bloc in course of India's freedom struggle. There was no bitterness or souring of relationship between Anna and Kejriwal because the ultimate goal of both was a clean and corruption free political dispensation. Anna himself had said while announcing the split in his movement that though their routes were different, their 'manjil' (goal) was the same. When Anna specifically prohibited the use of his name or photo by Kejriwal's political outfit, Kejriwal responded saying that Anna's photo was in his heart. That underlined the basic unity of heart and purpose between Anna and Kejriwal, even though they chose to proceed along different paths.

Looking back at the history of India's freedom struggle, a striking similarity is noticeable in the relationship between Gandhiji and Netaji Subhas Chandra Bose. It may be noted that Netaji set up the Provisional Government of Free India at Singapore in October 1943 and reorganised the Indian National Army (INA) in a big way. In 1944 summer, an INA battalion under the command of Captain Shah Nawaz launched its Imphal campaign inside the Indian border. It was around this time that Netaji made his famous broadcast on Azad Hind Radio addressed to Gandhiji : "India's last war of independence has begun. *Father of our Nation*, in this holy war of India's liberation, we ask for your blessings and good wishes." That highlights the deep regard Netaji had for Gandhiji and unity of purpose between them. Kejriwal's regard for Anna was somewhat similar even though he chose to proceed along a different route.

The leading civil society activists accompanying Kejriwal when he announced the formation of his political party included Prashant Bhushan, Shanti Bhushan, Yogendra Yadav, Manish Sisodia, Kumar Bishwas and Gopal Rai. Kumar Bishwas made a significant observation pregnant with great possibilities. He asserted that he had come to Kejriwal's platform as an outsider and would not join his party. For if ever Kejriwal's party strayed away from the right path, he would hit the street along with common people to oppose and protest against it.

That sounds nice, as eternal vigilance by the people is necessary to keep political parties glued to the straight path and prevent the political class from falling prey to the temptations of power. But 'eternal vigilance' should not be equated with chronic street protests by one group or another according to its own perception of what is the right path and what is not. For a political system cannot survive and a society cannot flourish in a state of perpetual street protests raging and tearing on one pretext or another.

The Chinese communist dictator, Mao believed in and practiced this dangerous course of "perpetual revolution" to keep his party and cadres on what he held to be the right path. To check the growing disillusionment among the Chinese people and his own party cadres with his economic policies. Mao resorted to a tearing and splitting campaign for what he called a 'cultural transformation' beginning 1966. Masses of young students backed by the People's Liberation Army were organised into revolutionary Red Guards to terrorise and demolish party functionaries and cadres who did not quite agree with Mao's prescriptions Blamed for "taking the capitalist road" the dissenting communist cadres' were attacked, humiliated in public and physically incapacitated in the name of the "Great Proletarian Cultural Revolution." The victims including Deng Xiaoping who somehow survived the ordeal. But by the time the so-called "cultural revolution" ended in 1969, the Chinese society was in ruins. It was left to the lone notable survivor-Deng Xiaoping-to shape the destiny of China in post Mao era. Ironically, China today is hurtling along the same "capitalist road" which was sought to be demolished through the great "Cultural Revolution".

That was a digression to illustrate the point that no society can live in a state of perpetual "revolution" as Mao propounded and practiced. As regards Kejriwal's prescription of simple and austere living of his would-be party legislators, there is nothing new or original about it. A glance at the exhilarating scenario of austerity on the part of politicians when Congress Ministries were formed in several Provinces in 1937 under the scheme of limited Provincial Autonomy would be relevant here. When politicians in Khadi, which was a symbol of purity and self sacrifice, who had adorned British Indian Jails during freedom struggle, occupied the seats of power, it appeared to have ushered in the dawn of a new era of clean politician. When Congress Ministers decided to work on salaries of Rs. 500 per month, as against Rs. 2000 - which they were entitled to, it eloquently sentdown the message of austere living and service spirit.

But what happened? The Congress Ministries remained in power for 28 months only. That was good enough to expose the chinks in their armour. The scramble for jobs and positions of personal benefits leading to corruption in the ranks of the ruling party became the order of the day. As referred to in chapter 8, the venerable. Father of the Nation was so perturbed about it that he felt like disbanding the Congress organisation "rather than put up with the corruption that is rampant." That was a fact recorded in history and history cannot be wished away. If anything, appropriate lesson has to be taken from history which is an authentic guide for course of action by succeeding generations.

That is not to downplay or deflate the noble aspirations of high flying young idealists represented by Kejriwal and Co. out to transform the severely flawed political system to usher in a new millennium. Far from it. It is only a cautionary reminder for the protagonists of the new political party aspiring to bring about a revolutionary change in the existing system. With all their high idealism, they have to guard against the pit falls of the past. It was in this view of political reality that Anna, while disassociating himself from the political party line, observed that "politics is full of dirt." And Anna was not far wrong. For the way politics is practiced in our country, it can safely be said that politics corrupts and pure politics without idealism corrupts absolutely.

That again is not to detract from the high moral pedestal sought to be occupied by Kejriwal and his associates in their mission to change the status quo for the better. The agenda of the proposed political party released by Kejriwal on 2nd October 2012 was overtly revolutionary.

Manish Sisodia, the other half of Kejriwal's movement, affirmed that their political party would be built "from the bottom up"-in respect of everything like selection of party candidates, funding, choice of development projects etc. In the backdrop of India's socio-economic and political complexities, that was truly Utopian. And Utopias are and have always been the pious dreams of great revolutionaries in all times and times which are hardly attainable.

As a scribe put it, no such dream of great revolutionaries the world over has ever been fulfilled. As Arnold Toyanbee, the renowned western historian put it, the Marxian Vision of a classless society was the greatest Utopia of the 20th century. But by the end of the 20th century, that Utopia was in ruins. Instead of the state "withering away" in accordance with the Marxian prognosis, it turned out to be a monstrous Leviathan throwing up dictators like Stalin and Mao. In fact, the term "Utopian" has come to be equated with impracticable in common parlance. For instance, when Kejriwal says that prices of essential commodities would be determined by the common man, it not only seems impracticable but fails to make any sense. For elementary economics postulates that price of a commodity is determined by the interplay of demand and supply. Price control of essential commodities by governmental agencies is well known but how can the so called 'common man' control prices?

Such patently inconvenient question marks on their utopian agenda were conveniently put under the carpet by Kejriwal and Co. while launching their party from a high political pedestal. It cannot be imagined that they were not conscious about the impractability of many of their promises on the ground. But they evidently chose to ignore it to score a point over all other political parties. In other words, they started with a game of one upmanship as they entered the political arena out to dwarf, if not demolish, all other political parties, in power or in opposition. A tall order by all account. In that sense, the policy document of Kejriwal's upcoming political party can be appropriately described as populist rather than realist or practicable. It was evidently aimed at garnering popular support in electoral politics.

Simultaneously with his jump into politics, Kejriwal continued with his campaign of exposing weak spots of established political parties by hurling corruption charges against their leadership. With the media ever eager to lap it up, Kejriwal hogged the limelight at the expense of the other political party leaders targeted by him. In this campaign, his background as a leading RTI activist, for which he had received international recognition earlier, came in handy. And there was a method in his exposure of politicians of different parties. He collected materials against them from diverse sources first and then charged them publicly. And that, again, not in one go but in installments to have the maximum impact. The idea was to tarnish the image of the established parties and send the message that his was the only anti-corruption party committed to the good of the common man. Interestingly, Kejriwal wears a cap inscribed with the slogan "I am a common man." (Earlier it used to be "I am Anna"). Through strategically calibrated revealations of alleged corruption or misconduct of politicians at regular intervals, Kejriwal managed to remain in the news, which is the hallmark of a successful politician. Prodded by self assessment based on Face Book and SMSs, he was optimistic about his media hyped new born party emerging as the political alternative to the established parties. He was confident that when his party candidates, meticulously selected on the basis of their incorruptible and clean image committed to the service of common man were pitted against tainted politicians of other parties, they would be the voters' choice in any election.

The major road block in the way of Kejriwal's party emerging as the political alternative is its entirely city-based activism. And that also in an around the national capital. His targets of attack so far have been the two national parties-Congress and the BJP- which constitute the power center at Delhi. There is a method in that also. He seems to believe that once he succeeds in causing significant erosion in the image and electoral prospect of the two national parties at Delhi, it would have a multiplier effect throughout the country. To say the least, that is a wild assumption which could be wide off the mark. For any political movement which leaves the vast hinterland interland of rural India untouched is doomed to fail. More so in case of a fledgeling political party which aspires to emerge as the political alternative in India.

Kejriwal & Co. seem to be banking on the chequered history of India in the past when once a conqueror captured Delhi, the whole country, or a major part of it, came under his sway. That past is now buried in history. India today is a vibrant democracy with an awakened people asserting their right aggressively to elect their rulers. The federal structure of power sharing between the Center and States has thrown up powerful regional satraps calling the shots in their respective states. In such a multiple power structure with rural and urban voters at the base, any Delhi-centric political adventure cannot hope to dislodge or replace the established national parties.

How then Kejriwal's new avatar as a crusading political leader would impact the political scenario in the short term? In other words, what would be its political fallout on the existing power structure? The answer is twofold. First, his effort to occupy the space which legitimately belongs to the major opposition party might partially succeed in certain areas. Like in Delhi where the two national parties - the ruling Congress and opposition BJP- are pitted against each other. By aggressively attacking the ruling Congress party with allegations of corruption, which should and could have normally been done by the opposition BJP, he might steal a march over the latter in electoral terms. To that extent, his foray in electoral politics might cause a dent in BJP's challenge to the ruling Congress party by splitting the opposition vote in the next election in Delhi. But no more.

Second, and more important, Kejriwal's relentless tirade against the ruling Congress party on charges of corruption would severely damage the prospect of the UPA Government and the Congress Party in elections country wide. By hurling allegations of corruption against the ruling party, already over-burdened with scams like 2G Spectrum, Coalgate, etc., at regular intervals, Kejriwal's unrelenting campaign has kept the pot boiling at the cost of the UPA Government and its lead Congress Party. He has thus hijacked the a political Lokpal-centric anti-corruption movement started by the Gandhian Anna Hazare to project his new party as the political alternative. How far he would succeed in his political adventure is in the womb of the future. One thing, however, has to be kept in mind while assessing the prospect of his political enterprise. Any amount of negative political exercise which he has been indulging in apart, of course, from his utopian promises, was not likely to bring up a positive political alternative on its own.

24

The Show Goes on

Any movement against corruption cannot come to a full stop. It is bound to be and has to be a long drawn out and continuing process. "Eternal vigilance is the price of liberty' is a well known adage. In the same sense, 'eternal vigilance' is the watch-word to keep corruption in check, if not to eradicate it altogether.

Endemic corruption, like when a litigant pays tips to a court clerk for obtaining copy of a document needed in his case, does not hurt anybody. Similarly, payment of "speed money" to a low key government functionary for expediting action otherwise legitimate hardly comes under the purview of an anti-corruption exercise. With vastly increased scope and scale of governmental activity affecting the economic life of the common man, the dimension of corruption has also expanded vastly. Be it the Indira Awas Yojna or Mahatma Gandhi National Rural Employment Guarantee Programme, the entire delivery mechanism of welfare measures meant for the people has become tainted with rampant corruption.

In a sense, that kind of corruption at the middle and grass root level can also be dubbed as endemic corruption which has long been a part of our socio-economic life. Though it adversely impacts the rural poor, it is only a minor part of the corruption syndrome of India. It is corruption of greater magnitude involving the higher echelons of administrative machinery that is targeted by the on-going anti-corruption movement rocking the country.

For corruption travels from top to bottom and not the other way round. And, as discussed earlier, the higher economic growth rate of India consequent upon the open door liberal economic policy beginning the last decade of the last century, has, ironically, widened the scope of corruption at the top level of governance.

The British colonial rulers were the earliest to recognise the prevalence of corruption in the flawed Indian socio-economic life. Lord Cornwallis who came to India to clean up the mess created by rapacious officers of East India Company headed by Lord Clive articulated it when he observed: "Every native of Hindustan, I verily believe, is corrupt." Evidently he was referring to endemic corruption of the kind mentioned above. But that was peanuts in comparison to the corruption indulged in by his own country's empire builders Warren Hastings and Robert Clive as colonial rulers of India. Both enriched themselves hugely through corrupt practices in India as East India Company's representatives and both had to face Parliamentary enquiry on return to England.

Robert Clive defended himself with characteristic gusto claiming that, in view of the temptation before him in India, he was rather modest in his acquisitions. His defence was based on the assertion that corruption was a way of life in India. That was only an incidental outburst of Clive in course of his defence, which did not cut much ice in the Parliamentary enquiry. Clive was let off the hook by British Parliament for other reasons. He had out-done his French rival Duplex in the game of empire building in India. By conquering South India, he had transformed a mere trading company into a ruling territorial power. In the words of Lord Macaulay, "Such an extent of cultivated territory, such an amount of revenue, such a multitude of subjects, was never added to the dominion of Rome by the most successful pro-consul......." In those days of expanding British imperialism, he was hailed as a hero for aiding the process which allowed him to escape indictment by British Parliament.

While Clive got away with his personal corruption in the wake of his successful empire building efforts, his successor-Warren Hastings-was not so lucky. He had continued with Clive's corrupt practice of using his office to make money for himself. According to one estimate, his personal accumulations from gifts and bribes amounted to around Rs. 30 lakhs a fabulous amount over two hundred years ago. Edmund Burke led a crusade against him in British Parliament and in 1780, the House of Commons passed a resolution for his recall from India. But he continued at the helm in India till 1785 by bribing the Directors of East India Company and showering favours on their kith and kin. On his return from India, he was impeached by the British Parliament and the trial lasted from 1788 to 1795.

Although Warren Hastings was ultimately acquitted by the Parliament in consideration of his services to British Empire, the protracted trial, specially Edmind Barke's scathing criticism of his corrupt practices in India, left its indelible mark on the course of British rule in India. His successor, Lord Cornwallis was not only himself above corruption but initiated measures to eradicate bribery, corruption and evils of private trade by Company's employees. He required each officer of the Company to declare his assets under oath before leaving India and enforced it strictly, dismissing some high officials in the process. He also struck at the basic incongruity of meager emoluments and high responsibility which led to corruption on the part of Company's employees by raising salaries commensurate with responsibility.

Evidently his remark about endemic corruption of "every native of Hindustan" was his reaction to the ease with which his predecessors - Clive and Warren Hastings - made money during their tenure in India. But there is an ominous ring of truth in his rather casual remark which haunts us today. Even the notoriously corrupt Robert Clive's assertion, in his defence in course of the Parliamentary enquiry against him, that corruption was a way of life in India sticks. What Robert Clive meant to convey was that temptation to amass wealth through corruption in India was so great that he was surprised at his own moderation.

That brings out another reality of the Indian situation. So much is being done to bring about necessary improvement in the infrastructure sector like roads, railways, civil aviation, telecommunication, power generation, etc., involving contracts and deals worth huge sums of money. This is growing and is bound to grow by the day in order to meet the growing requirement of the country in the infrastructure sector. And where there is a deal involving lacs of crores of rupees, it is open to corruption on a large scale. For, a certain percentage of the money involved in any project is built into any deal to be paid as bribe in order to clinch the deal. Every contractor or executing agent of any project big and small - knows this and so does the government functionary empowered to award the contract. That is the dark area of temptation to indulge in corruption on the part of powers that be arising out of much needed infrastructure development in India. With so much money on offer in normal course, it is difficult to resist the temptation to be corrupt.

But Robert Clive's swash-buckling remark that corruption was a way of life in India was not made in the above context. For there was no such development effort or money on offer in India at that time. On the other hand, the rapacious minions of East India Company were cutting every corner to establish the British Empire in India and enrich themselves in the process. In the circumstances, Clive's sweeping comment on corruption in India was more a diversionary move in his defence before Parliament than a statement of reality. It was like takers of huge amounts as dowry in arranged marriages in our country passing the buck on the givers of dowry. For the likes of Robert Clive and Warren Hastings, any opening was good enough to make money by corrupt means. For instance, Warren Hastings extorted bribes of Rs. 2 lakhs from Raja Chait Singh of Benaras and Rs. 10 lakhs from the Nawab of Oudh on the plea of financing the Maratha wars.

In present day India, it is our own home grown Robert Clives and Warren Hastings who have pushed the country into the mire of corruption. As a result, corruption scandals have been not only raining but pouring in torrents in recent years - 2G Spectrum, Common wealth Games, 'Coalgate' and what have you. Wherever you put your finger, you are likely to touch a scam. In fact, there has been a corruption explosion in India today like never before. And this has ignited an explosion of anti-corruption movement country wide on a scale also as never before. J.P's anti-corruption campaign of 1970's was largely confined to Gujarat and Bihar. The anti-corruption stir started by Anna Hazare in April 2011 has spread across the board through out the country. J.P's movement jumped the board of corruption and adopted a wide socio-political reform agenda termed as 'Total Revolution'. The current anti-corruption movement remains primarily focused on eradication of corruption, even though both Anna Hazare and Arvind Kejriwal have also been talking about ancillary electoral reforms like right to recall and right to reject.

In any case, J.P's anti-corruption movement came to an abrupt end with the imposition of Emergency by Indira Gandhi in June 1975. At the end of the Emergency in January 1977, J.P. re-emerged on the India scene in his new avatar as a giant crusader for democracy which was sought to be eclipsed by Indira Gandhi through the Emergency regime. But his focus was shifted from the issue of corruption to restoration of political democracy in India in the wake of the harrowing experience of the Emergency regime. He remained engaged in rounding off the angularities and resolving the clash of personalities of political leaders who came to power in the spring of 1977 until the end of his life in October 1979.

This time round, the anti-corruption movement refuses to fade away, even though slowing down at times and picking up momentum again. The pitch of the movement is sometimes high, sometimes low, but the movement as such continues unabated. For the simple reason that corruption scandals continue to surface time after time with ominous regularity. Hardly have the weilders of power a breather from sustained attack of anti-corruption activists when a scandal erupts out of the blue to shake them up. And a hyper active media, which is a sine qua non of a vibrant democracy, always on an over-drive, keeps them on tenterhooks. In kind of a Newtonian reaction, the anti-corruption activists push forward their crusade with renewed vigour as the stream of corruption continues to flow unchecked.

After lying low for some time to recharge himself physically, the octogenarian anti-corruption man for all seasons-Anna Hazare-came up with a bang to give a new phillip to his movement. Looking fresh after his self-imposed silence for a few months, he addressed an impressive rally of around 25,000 enthusiastic supporters at

Patna's historic Gandhi Maidan on 30 January 2013 vowing to accomplish the unfinished tasks of his anti-graft movement launched in April 2011. Adding glamour to the rally, the former Army Chief (Retired) General V.K. Singh, Kiran Bedi and senior journalists Santosh Bhartia kept waving the National Flag from the dias while Anna was addressing the rally. The date and venue of the rally were specifically selected to lend an aura of sacredness to it on two counts. First, 30th January was the date of Mahatma Gandhi's martyrdom and second Patna was the place from where J.P. had launched his grand movement in defence of democracy in 1977. Significantly enough, the rally was termed as *"Jantantra Rally"*. On this occasion, a book entitled *"Uprising 2011"* was also released by Anna along with Kiran Bedi and General (Retd.) V.K. Singh.

At the rally, Anna announced launching of a new front entitled *"Jantantra Morcha"* to pursue and achieve such unfinished agenda of his movement as passage of Jan Lok Pal Bill. Right to Recall and Reject, Empowerment of Gram Sabhas, strengthening of the Right to Information Act for bringing about a complete change in the existing system of governance. Continuing with his tirade against the Government, he said that the powers that be were not interested in passing the Lok Pal Bill because 163 MPs were dented with corruption charges. "Atleast 15 Ministers of the UPA Government would be put behind bars" he added, "if our Jan Lok Pal Bill is enacted in Parliament". Highlighting the apolitical nature of his movement, Anna declared that he or any other member of his "Jantantra Morcha" would not contest any election, thus separating his "Morcha" from his erstwhile colleague Arvind Kejriwal's *"Am Admi Party."* But he emphasised that corruption could not be rooted out unless voters were empowered with legal provisions like right to recall and right to reject. The present flawed system of governance, he claimed, could not be changed without required electoral reforms.

Encouraged by the cheers of a sizeable crowd, Anna administered a pledge to the people asking them to take a resolve to fight against corruption through all non-violent means. He thundered : "I will mobilise at least six crore people and bring them under one platform so that they can act as a pressure group on the government as any dispensation fears from crumbling down under the people's pressure." Making a passing reference to the coal blocks allocation scam, he declared that his people would go to the general masses to acquaint them with the scam. Those who shared the dais with Anna included, besides General (Retd) V.K. Singh and Kiran Bedi, P.V. Rajagal, founder of Ekta Parishad and Rajendra Singh, "Waterman of Rajasthan".

Nitish Kumar, the Chief Minister of Bihar where the rally was held, applauded Anna for his anti-corruption initiative and sustained crusade. He also expressed his support for Anna on issues like Right to Reject and Right to Recall. He agreed with Anna that successive governments formed in the wake of J.P.'s movement left several tasks unfinished which need to be completed.

By calling his Patna meeting "Jantantra Rally" and christening his new outfit as "Jantantra Morcha", Anna sought to take his new initiative a notch higher to include electoral reforms in his agenda, apart from enactment of Jan Lok Pal Bill. Apparently, it was on the lines of J.P. movement which started as an anti-corruption agitation and culminated in his call for "*Total Revolution*" encapsuling a wide range of socio-political reforms. Since he had consciously selected J.P.'s "*karmbhoomi*" to launch his new initiative, he sought to emulate J.P. in widening the range of his agenda to make it appear more hallowed and holy in the eyes of the people. But inspite of this exercise at window-dressing, Anna's movement, now termed as "Jantantra Morcha", remained out and out an anti-corruption crusade as it was when started in April 2011. The inclusion of necessary electoral reforms in Anna's agenda was only incidental to his movement focused on the fight against corruption.

Anna loudly proclaimed the apolitical or non-political character of his movement when he declared that no member of his organisation would contest any election. It was on this issue that his one-time trusted colleague and most visible torch-bearer Arvind Kejriwal parted company with him in September-October 2012. To make his overtly political initiative attractive, Kejriwal unfolded an Utopian vision document incorporating a wide range of populist goals alongwith a code of conduct for his party men calculated to win over the common people. Anna resorted to no such gimmic. His movement, despite its new name, remained solely embedded to eradication of corruption with necessary incidental reforms.

In his fresh initiative, Anna got a new heavy weight associate in General (Retd) V.K. Singh. It was General V.K. Singh who moved around Bihar and stationed himself at Patna in preparation for the 30th January 2013 "Jantantra Rally" addressed by Anna. The ex-Army Chief was already on board with Anna's band-wagon from the moment of his retirement. It was he who had offered a glass of juice to Anna to break his fast at Jantar Mantar on 4th August 2012 when he lambasted the "rampant corruption" pushing the country downhill. By January 2013, the retired General had emerged as another stalwart in the lead of the anti-corruption movement in the country.

His jumping into the wave of anti-corruption movement was not a freak post-retirement enterprise. General V.K. Singh was on the same wave length as the anti-corruption activists even before he openly aligned with Anna in the anti-corruption movement. In early 2012, General Singh had alleged that he was offered a bribe of Rs. 14 crores to clear a tranche of 600 'substandard' Tatra Trucks for use in the Army through a subordinate Lt. General. When he objected to it and rejected the offer, the Lt. General told him that there was nothing wrong in it as it was a done thing in the Army. When Gen. V.K. Singh's allegation became public, the concerned Lt. General even dragged him to court in a defamation suit. The Tatra Truck Scam pertained to alleged shady dealings between BEML and British firm, Tatra Sipox. Reportedly, more than Rs. 750 crores was siphoned off over a period of ten years. The scam was referred to CBI for investigation nearly two months after it was highlighted by the media.

That, incidentally, brings up the issue of another area of darkness in the overall corruption scenario of the country. That is the secretive world of contracts and deals related to procurement of defence equipments. In fact, the defence sector is the most vulnerable area for corrupt deals, for the simple reason that all processes and contracts are shrouded in secrecy, supposedly in the interest of the Country's security. The participation of middle man in defence deals is well known. It is also an open secret that a certain percentage of the deal amount is earmarked by armament firms as commission to middlemen. That leaves enough room for payment of hefty commission by the supplier company to middlemen for clinching the deal. And in so doing, the middlemen have to dole out a part of the commission money to the government functionaries empowered to approve the deal. It may be noted that India is a big market for arms manufacturers of the world who jostle with each other to win over multi-crore deals for supply of their ware to the country. And in the hallowed area of defence, contracts for weapons and equipments run into hundreds or thousands of crores. One can imagine the amount of bribe money on offer in defence purchases corrupting the entire process of defence deals.

This is true of all major contracts and deals, as mentioned earlier, in infrastructure development sector with one significant difference. While all deals in other sectors are carried out in the open, a veil of secrecy surrounds all transactions in the defence sector, which makes it the most convenient arena for free play of corrupt practices. In one case of recent years, the media somehow uncovered the veil of secrecy and exposed the irregularities involved in a deal which forced the government to act. This was the deal for 197 light utility helicopters worth over Rs. 3000 crores for the Army in which Eurocopter had emerged as the front-runner. When the media continued reporting about irregularities in the proposed deal, the government had to cancel it at the last moment in 2007 and opt for fresh tender.

It would be relevant here to refer to what *Transparency International* has to say about corruption index of India's defence sector. A report prepared by the U.K. chapter of Transparency Internal after nine years of research on 82 countries has placed India in the "High Corruption Risk" category. The report classifies 82 countries into six categories. These are :- Category A termed as "Very Low Corruption Risk", Category B termed as Low

Corruption Risk", Category C known as "Moderate Corruption Risk", Category D called "High Corruption Risk", Category E denoting "Very High Corruption Risk" and Category F termed as "Critical Corruption Risk". The Report places India in Category D alongwith several other countries namely China, Pakistan, Bangladesh, Turkey, Malaysia, Ethiopia etc.

It is no consolation that countries like China and Pakistan have also been clubbed together with India in this "High Corruption Risk' group. Neither is it a matter of comfort that countries like Afghanistan, Saudi Arabia, Iran, Iraq, Sri Lanka, etc., have been placed in "Very High Corruption Risk' group and still others like Libya, Syria and Egypt further down in "Critical Corruption Risk" group. Considering the vast defence market of India, which is much bigger in size and population than Pakistan, Bangladesh and Malaysia, the "High Corruption Risk" category is bad enough to cause serious concern. For a large part of India's defence requirements is met by foreign arms manufacturers who tend to indulge in shady deals. As far as China is concerned, it is itself a big weapons producing country not so much dependent on foreign suppliers as India. The Transparency International's report has placed China in a "High Corruption Risk" category primarily because of lack of meaningful scrutiny of its secret defence budgets. There is no dearth of regulations to control corruption risk in China, but the concentration of power in the highly centralized administrative structure itself creates corruption risk. In any case, the fact that my neighbour is corrupt cannot hide or minimise the guilt of my own corruption.

Commenting further on D Category ("High Corruption Risk") countries, in which India is placed, the Transparency International Report says that these countries lack a proper system for whistle blower protection and control over expenditure on secret items and programmes. They do not have adequate legislature scrutiny on defence expenditure. As kind of a sweetener, the report concedes that India is the only country in this category which has some controls to check sub-contractors in defence procurement.

In the foreword of Transparency International's Report, the Director Mark Pyman observes: "We have found that many senior defence officials, senior officers and ministers are aware of the corruption risks in defence. They know that public trust is important, and that secrecy and corruption scandals damage that trust. They know that corruption corrodes operational effectiveness and means that their soldiers are at risk when deployed with inappropriate or faulty equipment. They are aware that the temptation of large bribes can lead to unnecessary purchases. They are conscious of what a huge waste of money such corruption can be".

Though a generalised observation on corruption in defence sector in different countries, it could be true of India's defence establishment as well. And yet corruption continues to plague India's defence sector as evident from scams and scandals coming to the surface from time to time. The latest to hit the headlines is Augusta Westland Chopper scam which has raised a storm in the country. More about it in the next chapter.

Corruption in defence sector, highlighted by the recent report of Transparency International referred to above, is only a part of the corruption story. It cannot divert people's attention from widespread corruption in every other sector of governance. As it was raining scams and scandals day after day, the corruption issue that led to wide spread protests in 2011 has not faded away. Nor is it likely to fade away in near future. For nothing tangible has been done to bring about the required institutional clean up. Not a single systemic reform to promote transparent public procurement in defence and other sectors, non-discretionary allocation of resources like coal blocks, strict social audit of public fund spending or well targeted and flawless delivery of services has been brought about. The Government's only answer to mounting public outrage at unstoppable corruption scandals is knee-jerk reaction like moratorium on defence purchases and blacklisting of manufacturing firms. CBI, the premier anti-corruption agency, remains mired in controversy allegedly as a political trouble-shooter of the government in power. It may be recalled that one of the essential reforms demanded by anti-corruption activists is to free the CBI from the control of the party in power in order to make it an effective instrument to curb corruption.

In the circumstances, the stream of corruption continues to flow unchecked inundating the country. As a natural reaction, the wave of protests by anti-corruption activists, social and political, continues to sweep the land. The flame of anti-corruption movement ignified by Anna Hazare in April, 2011 continues to burn and engulf the country. As the demon of corruption stalks the land, the stage is set for a long drawn-out crusade against it. The principal actors on the anti-corruption stage-Anna Hazare, Arvind Kejriwal, Kiran Bedi and now General (Retd.) V.K. Singh, hailed as redeemers of an awfully flawed system, continue to keep the issue of corruption alive and hot, as the show goes on. And, as they say, the show goes on.

Arvind Kejriwal, the inveterate protester against anything smacking of corruption, and Anna Hazare, the indefatigable crusader against corruption, kept the show going. Kejriwal was at it again upping the ante against Delhi Government. Alleging that electricity and water bills issued to the citizens of Delhi were highly inflated due to corruption on the part of the authorities concerned, he sat on an 'indefinite' fast at Delhi in March, 2013 to register his protest. He had been repeatedly raising the issue of inflated power and water bills charging the Delhi Government with cheating the people. He had earlier made a show of tearing these bills and urging the citizens of Delhi to do the same and not to pay. He thereby sought to emulate Mahatma Gandhi's no-tax campaign during the freedom movement directed against the British colonial regime. Or at least, to revive memories of that and inspire the people to stand up against the allegedly corrupt dispensation.

It is another matter that Kejriwal's 'indefinite' fast in protest against 'inflated' bills this time round did not hog the limelight in the media. Nor did it meet with enthusiastic response from Delhiites. Not at least to the extent anticipated by Kejriwal and his associates. As a result Kejriwal broke his 'indefinite' fast after 14 days without any response or gesture from the Delhi Government authorities concerned. He, however, patted his own back for surviving on intake of water only for 14 days. And, more importantly, he claimed that by fasting, he had succeeded in highlighting the issue of inflated power and water bills as important electoral agenda for the

Assembly and Parliamentary elections in Delhi. That was quite in sync with his political ambitiom of winning elections in Delhi and projecting his *Aam Admi Party* as a viable political outfit.

On the other hand, Anna Hazare's apolitical or non-political crusade against corruption continued slowly but steadily. Anna set upon his *'Jantantra Yatra"* to arouse the people against corrupt politicians. Starting from Amritsar in March 2013, he and his team reached Jalandhar on the night of 31 March in course of his projected tour of the country. Unfased by relatively less impressive crowds attending his rally, he exhorted the voters to elect only clean candidates in the next elections and reject the corrupt and tainted ones. Without mincing words, he thundered that people vote the politicians to power in order to serve them and plan and improve their future. But once elected, the political power-wielders start looting and plundering the people. He emphasised that only such people should be entrusted with power who serve the people and not rule over them. For political leaders are supposed to be servants of the people and not their masters.

Anna and his team's 'Jantantra Yatra' was scheduled to cover the whole country in phases, as he had announced in the first 'Jantantra Rally' at Patna on 30 January 2013. Anna himself could not attend the next 'Jantantra Rally' as he was not physically fully fit. But the rally schedule was not disrupted. General (Retd) V.K. Singh was there to take the baton from Anna and address the rally.

In a broader sense, Anna's 'apolitical' campaign was also political because it was aimed at rejecting corrupt politicians by defeating them at the hustings and bringing up honest and clean people to occupy the seats of power. But it was non-political in the sense that Anna did not form a political party to contest elections on its own. In this respect, his anti-corruption movement was like J.P's, who had quit politics in 1954 itself but jumped into the fray before and after the 'Emergency' during 1970's first as an anti-corruption crusader and then as a saviour of democracy. Significantly enough, Anna called his projected countrywide tour as "Jantantra Yatra".

Arvind Kejriwal, on the other hand, formed an overt political outfit of his own known as '*Aam Admi Party*' out to contest election and capture the seats of power. But as observed earlier, their goal was the same, a corruption-free dispensation, though they took to different paths. Between the two of them - Anna Hazare and Arvind Kejriwal, they kept the flame of anti-corruption movement burning and the show going.

25

Augusta Westland Chopper Scam

They say it is a replication of Bofors Gun deal scandal that had erupted in 1987. It related to payment of bribes by the gun manufacturer, A.B. Bofors for securing an order from the Government of India to supply 155 mm howitzer guns for the armed forces. The Augusta Westland Chopper scam is so in a sense on two counts. First, like Bofors, it is one of the rare cases in which bribery has been detected and brought to light from the giver's end and not the taker's as normally happens in corruption cases. Second, it shares what can be called a common Italian connection as in the case of Bofors gun deal scam. In the case of Bofors, those accused of receiving bribe money included Ottavio Quattrocchi, a high profile Italian business representative operating in Delhi. The Italian connection was indirect in this case. In Augusta Westland scam, the bribe giving company is itself the U.K. subsidiary of Italian company Finmeccanica, thus pointing to direct Italian connection in the chopper scam.

But the similarity ends here. The Bofors deal scam related to purchase of 155 mm howitzer guns, a very vital requirement of Indian defence forces. It may be noted that the Bofors guns acquired through this deal came in handy and proved very useful during the Indo-Pakistan Kargil war. On the other hand, the Augusta Westland scam involves the purchase of helicopters for the use of India's V.V.I.P's, a relatively minor item in respect of its end use. Also, the amount of bribe paid in Bofors deal which came out in the open was less than the amount alleged to have been paid in the Augusta Westland Chopper deal. And yet, the Bofors gun scam so much rocked the country that the incumbent Prime Minister, Rajiv Gandhi came close to losing his Prime Ministership. The chopper scam was still in the process of unfolding itself and one could not predict where the buck would eventually stop.

But what actually is the Augusta Westland scam all about? It refers to Rs. 3,546 crores deal with Augusta Westland company for supply of 12 helicopters to be used by the President, Prime Minister and other VVIP's . The deal was signed by India's Defence Minister in 2010. At the time when the scam erupted, three helicopters, out of the 12 billed for, had arrived with some initial spare parts just enough to fly for a few months and nearly 45 per cent of the money had already been paid. In the process, bribes of 51 million Euros (about Rs. 370 crores) were paid in Italy and India to clinch the deal. It is the payment of kickbacks of about Rs. 370 crores for securing the purchase order from the India government which is crux of the scam. And it was not only a rare case like Bofors gun deal, in which the fact of bribery for clinching the deal came to light from the giver's end, but also perhaps the first time that a bribe giver had named the bribe takers and spelt out the services they provided. But when did it come to light in India?

It erupted in India in a big way only when the arrest of Giuseppe Orsi, the CEO of Finmeccanica, the parent company of Augusta Westland, on corruption charges hogged the headlines in the Indian media in February, 2013. It was a hot news with an element of surprise because, as mentioned earlier, it was a unique case in which the bribe giver, and not the taker, was being hauled up and put behind the bars. Once the news broke out, the media was flooded with information about the facts of the case including the ground of arrest of the Finmeccanica CEO Orsi. It transpired that Italian prosecutors had in a report filed in the tribunal of Busto Arsizio city on 12 February, 2012 alleged that the Italian business conglomerate had bribed the Indian authorities concerned to swing the deal in its favour. The report revealed that kickbacks of 51 million Euros (about Rs. 370 crore) were paid in Italy and India through intermediaries. The report even named some close relatives of a former Indian Air Force Chief who allegedly received the kickbacks. The Italian prosecutors' report claimed that alleged middlemen Guido Haschke, Carlo Gerosa, and Christian Michel facilitated the payments to the Indians concerned.

According to the documents submitted in Italian court, the total bribe money was estimated at 51 million Euros. Out of this amount, 30 million Euros were paid to the alleged U.K. based middleman, Christian Michel for payment to Italian politicians. At least 21 million Euros were sent to India via Tunisia between 2007 and 2011. The bribe money was delivered in the name of fake engineering contracts routed through the Tunisian firm IDS Tunisia "FDS India received theses sums of money in order to pay public officials in India," according to Italian documents. Further, one lakh Euros were paid directly in cash to the close relations of the former Indian Air Force Chief.

It may be noted here that the allegation of corruption in reverse, that is bribe giving, by Italy's own business conglomerate Finmeccanica, was being investigated by Italian agencies and even charge sheet was filed in court, but the over-vigilant Indian public remained blissfully unaware of it for over a year. How come? That brings out the ignorance of our anti-corruption activists, both social and political, and their superficial endeavours to pursue their own agenda. For whole one year from February 2012 to February 2013 when the Indian media brought it out of the Italian cupboard', anti-corruption activists in India had no clue about it. They were only beating about the bush and flogging a dead horse even though the Italian media had started reporting about the scam in February 2012 itself.

Arvind Kejriwal, who is always on the prowl to pick up any stick to attack the government on corruption issue, remained conspicuously silent on this latest scam because he had not cared to find it out even though it was being tossed around in the concerned government agencies. It had also escaped the radar of the veteran anti-corruption crusader Anna Hazare and his new found associate, General (Retd) V.K. Singh even though the Italian media was regularly reporting on the scandal. Till as late as 30 January 2013 when Hazare and V.K. Singh addressed a big anti-corruption rally at Patna, they did not touch upon it because they simply did not know. That is a sad commentary on the performance of our anti-corruption campaigners. It points to the lack of eternal vigilance which is the price of a clean and corruption free dispensation.

The silence of the anti-corruption activists is explained by their ignorance. Not so in case of the Indian government. With a full fledged Indian embassy operational at Rome and Italian agencies carrying forward their investigation against Augusta Westland under full public gaze, the Indian authorities could not have remained ignorant of it. If they slept over it for one full year, it was for other reasons. Badly hit by a flood of corruption scandals which refused to stop, with a raging anti-corruption stir shaking the country, the Indian government evidently tried to keep it under the carpet for as long as possible. Let the sleeping dogs lie seems to be the government's reaction to the unfolding of the scam by Italians.

Not that all was totally quiet on the government front though. The departments concerned were routinely going through the motions of taking cognizance of the scam without any meaningful effort to catch the bribe takers and prosecute them. In course of this half-hearted exercise, the Defence Secretary wrote to Secretary (West), Ministry of External Affairs in October 2012 to get information from the Italian authorities to enable the Defence Ministry to take further necessary action. He also requested the MEA to take up the matter with the U.K. government in view of the fact that the scam related to the U.K. company, Augusta Westland. In November 2012, the Secretary (West) MEA replied to the Defence Secretary saying that "the U.K. authorities were waiting for the results of the Italian investigation in order to ascertain whether there are further actions to take".

According to the Defence Ministry, its DG (Acquisition) sought a factual report in the matter from the Indian Embassy in Rome after the scam was first reported in the media in February 2012. In April, 2012 the Defence Ministry wrote again to the Indian Embassy in Rome seeking an update in the matter. The Defence Ministry said in a communique. "A detailed report on the status of the case was received from our Embassy in Rome in May 2012. The report made it clear that there are inherent difficulties in obtaining formal details of the case given the independence of the judiciary from the executive in Italy". In July 2012, the Defence Ministry wrote back to the Indian Embassy in Rome stating that it could approach the concerned judicial authorities directly. Accordingly, a formal request was actually made by the Embassy to the Naples prosecutor's office on 16 July 2012.

Evidently, the matter stopped at that. The action remained limited to futile triangular correspondence involving the Ministries of Defence and External Affairs and the Indian Embassy in Rome. According to one report another government agency the Central Vigilance Commission had also received a complaint about corruption involved in the chopper deal around the middle of 2012 and had referred it to the Chief Vigilance Officer of the Defence Ministry for a report. Meanwhile, the Italian media kept reporting on the middlemen involved in the deal and their Indian connection. According to the Italian newspaper "Lettera 43", the main commission agent, Christian Michel and another Guido Ralph Hascke had close Indian connection. In its report on 20 November 2012, the Italian paper reported that the "mysterious" British citizen Michel had received 60 per cent of the kickback amount of 51 million Euros from the manufacturer of Augusta Westland Choppers.

It is evident that the Italian media continued to throw light on the scam and its beneficiaries from their end without any meaningful response by the Indian authorities throughout the year 2012. The concerned authorities in India lulled themselves by indulging in routine correspondence with each other without the seriousness the matter deserved. The triangular correspondence among the Defence and External Affairs Ministries and the Indian Embassy in Rome was a typical example of bureaucratic jugglery passing on the buck from one to the other with no tangible outcome. With the result that the scam remained hidden under the carpet until it was uncovered by the media in India which flashed it in a big way in February 2013.

There was a shady background to the engagement between the Westland Helicopter Company and the Indian government. Way back in 1986, the Indian government signed a deal with a British company known as Westland Helicopters for the supply of 21 civilian choppers, even though these were not considered suitable for use in India only a year earlier. In March 1986, the then Minister of State for Civil Aviation said in Parliament: "Government has decided to purchase 21 Westland Helicopters to cater to the requirements of the petroleum sector and for scheduled/non-scheduled services provided by the Helicopter Corporation of India." The delivery of helicopters was to begin in May 1986 and completed by February 1988. Two of these helicopters met with accident in August 1988 and February 1989. When another helicopter of the lot met with a serious accident in December 1989, the Westland fleet was grounded. An expert committee was set up by the Government to examine the overall serviceability performance and safety record of Westland Helicopters.

And yet, the Westland fleet was re-inducted in September 1990 with reduced payload and utilisation rate. But the defect rate continued to be higher with the result that another aircraft of the Westland fleet met with an accident in December 1990. This compelled the DGCA to go into the viability of operations of these helicopters for which a sub-committee was appointed. It found that not only the Westland Company was not addressing the technical problems indicated in the earlier Expert Committee Report, but a new range of defects had come up. Most of these defects had flight safety implications. Accordingly, the sub-committee considered continued operation of Westland Helicopters unsafe and highly uneconomical. On the sub-committee's recommendation, the entire fleet of Westland Helicopters was grounded by the government in February 1991.

The economics of the use of these helicopters by the Helicopter Corporation of India was reviewed by the CAG. Its report covering the period up to March 1992 said : "As against the proposal submitted before Public Investment Board estimating a loss of Rs. 4.30 crores in the first year of operation of the helicopters and profit thereafter, the company suffered a loss of

Rs. 23.32 crores in the operation of Westland fleet from 1986-87 to 1990-91 due to high cost of operation and under utilisation". In April 2002, the then Civil Aviation Minister (in the N.D.A. government) admitted that during the period of operation of Westland Helicopters, Pawan Hans Helicopters Limited incurred an operational loss of Rs. 33.97 crores and aggregate loss of 95.67 crores.

Summing up the position, the Minister said: "The issue of overall performance of Westland Helicopters was taken up with the British government on many occasions. However, inspite of best efforts, no satisfactory solution could be found for various technical problems in the operation/maintenance of Westland Helicopters. As a result, it was decided to ground the entire fleet with effect from 09.02.1991." That proclaimed the inglorious end of a shady transaction involving the British Westland Helicopters Company.

More of it a little later, but first how was this U.K. based company connected with the Italian Augusta Westland Chopper company involved in the latest corruption scandal? The fact is that Westland became August, Westland in July 2000 after the Italian conglomerate Finmeccanica and U.K. based GKN merged their respective helicopter subsidiaries Augusta and Westland Helicopters to form Augusta Westland Company with each holding 50 per cent share in this new corporate entity. And in 2004, the Italian business house Finmeccanica acquired the U.K. based GKN's stake in Augusta Westland, which became a fully owned subsidiary of the Italian conglomerate. Thus, the scam that erupted in 2012-2013 related to Augusta Westland Helicopters company fully owned by the Italian company Finmeccanica which was being investigated by the Italian authorities. It was this Augusta Westland Helicopter Company which was awarded the contract by the Indian Defence Ministry for supply of V.V.I.P. Choppers in February 2010. And it was the fact of bribe paid by this company to clinch the deal which was being investigated by Italian probe agencies.

Reverting back to the disastrous deal for supply of 21 helicopters by the original Westland Helicopter company signed in March 1986, which ended in February 1991, there was nothing right about it from beginning to end. The very fact that the Westland Chopper on offer was considered unfit by the then Prime Minister himself in 1985 made its acceptance a year later in 1986 quite suspicious. In fact, the PM Rajiv Gandhi told the Rajya Sabha in May 2, 1985: "It is short in one very crucial area which affects safety." And his assessment proved quite correct as corroborated by the Westland helicopters' inglorious record of one accident after another between 1988 and 1990 leading to the grounding of the entire fleet in 1991. Apart from that, the manner in which the deal for purchase of 21 helicopters was made cast suspicion over the very deal itself. It was said that the helicopters were required for the petroleum sector, (whatever that meant), and for services to be provided by the Helicopter Corporation of India. It was not clear for what exact use the Petroleum Sector required it. The supposed requirement of the Helicopter Corporation of India was even more dubious. As subsequently assessed by CAG, part of the losses incurred by the Helicopter Corporation of India in operating these helicopters was caused by under utilisation of helicopter services. The entire deal made in 1986 conveyed the impression that the target of buying 21 Westland helicopters was fixed before nand and the need for it was contrived after that to justify the transaction. An example of unnecessary purchase at the cost of the government exchequer for other reasons, which in itself smacked of bribery and corruption. The ultimate grounding of the entire fleet of Westland helicopters in 1991 confirmed that suspicion.

And yet, the benign minions of Defence Ministry signed a contract for supply of 12 V.V.I.P. choppers with the same discredited company in its new avatar as Augusta Westland in 2010. For Augusta Westland was nothing more or less than the old Westland helicopter company, the deal with which had ended in disaster. It was the old wine in a new bottle, only the ownership had changed. The Defence Ministry could not rightly plead ignorance about the disastrous record of Westland helicopters while signing the deal with the same company in 2010. In any cases ignorance of a fact which the Defence officials were supposed to know could be no excuse for signing the deal. That was bad enough, but the worst apprehension about corruption involved in the deal came true when Italian investigators found out about payment of kickbacks in this transaction. The investigation report filed in Italian court said that the CEO of Finmeccanica, Giuseppe Orsi and Augusta Westland CEO, Bruno Spagnolini, had paid 30 million Euros (Rs. 217 crores) to Christain Michel, the British middleman involved in the deal.

The August Westland Company had in fact set aside Rs. 270 crores for pay off to clinch the Rs. 3,700 crore chopper deal from India. Its bosses used a network of middlemen, Christian Michel being the foremost among them, to grease the palms of those in a position to influence the contract. It was out of this total that Michal was paid Rs. 217 crore to bag the order and implement the contract. The remarkable fact to note is that Italian agencies ripped open the practice of bribery and corruption by their own countrymen to secure a purchase order from a foreign country (India) which was economically beneficial to their country. Reacting to the arrest of Orsi, ex CEO of the Italian company Finmeccanica, for paying bribes to secure the chopper purchase order from India, Italy's three time former Prime Minister Silvio Berlusconi said that bribes were necessary in doing business globally.

In a televised interview, Berlusconi observed, "Bribes are a phenomenon that exists and it is useless to deny the existence of these necessary situations. These are not crimes. We are taking about paying a commission to someone in that country. Why, because those are the rules in that country." Italian news agency, ANSA quoted Berlusconi as saying that probes by Italian prosecutors into contracts Italian firms sign abroad were a form of "economic suicide." That underlines the significance of exposure of the Augusta Westland Chopper scam which was economically beneficial to their country by Italians themselves. No wonder that *Transparency International's* Global Report on Defence Sector Corruption, (quoted in the previous chapter) has placed Italy in *"Moderate Corruption Risk category"* against India's placement in *"High Corruption Risk"* category. That is, Italy was less open to corruption in defence deals than India. That is corroboratedly by the fact that Italians have in the recent past acted to catch and punish the practitioners of corruption, however high and mighty in public life, unlike in India, where corrupt public functionaries continue to flourish and prosper in spite of serious corruption charges flying against them.

In 1992, a Socialist Party official in Italy was arrested in Milan for taking a bribe on a cleaning contract in an old people's home. This set in motion an anti-corruption tsunami which swept away Italy's veteran political leaders belonging to major parties which had shared power from time to time. The notable political figures who fell by the way-side included the Socialist leader Bettino Craxi, a former long-lasting Prime Minster of Italy and the Christian Democrat party leader Giulio Andreotti. And the public opinion in Italy loudly supported and hailed the punishment meted out to corrupt public functionaries. *"The Economist"* (London, dated 20 February 1993) reported, "Last Saturday night, the good citizens of cheity, a little town in central Italy, turned out to celebrate the arrest of their Mayor and half the town council on corruption charges, by uncorking bottles outside the local prison."

Digressing a little from corruption scenario in Italy and India, a glance at the Japanese response to corrupt practices in the recent past. Incidently, Japan is also clubbed with Italy in "Moderate Corruption Risk" category in Defence Sector by the Transparency International, referred to earlier. In 1989, a former Prime Minister of Japan. Noboru Takeshita, was forced to resign after exposure of Recruit shares-for-favours scandal. That proved to be the beginning of the end of Liberal Demoractic Party as the most powerful political outfit of Japan. The next notable political leader to bite the dust was Shin Kanemaru who, as the head of the ruling L.D.P's largest faction, wielded enormous power and was regarded as the king-maker. He admitted to have taken 4.2 million dollars from Sagawa Kyubin, a delivery firm with gangster connection, and had to bow out of office and politics in October 1992. In Japan's national election held in July 1993, the scandal scarred Liberal Democratic Party lost its majority for the first time since 1955.

That is how mature nations handle the scourge of corruption on the part of political power wielders without any damage to their country's progress and development. They catch and punish the corrupt, however high and mighty, with the whole hearted support of their people. And they are none the worse for it. In fact, the ignominious rejection of the corrupt politicians and their cohorts by the anti-corruption mechanism of their system of governance and by the people at large purifies their system and improves the quality of governance across the board.

In India, on the other hand, the hand that is supposed to catch and punish the corrupt wielders of power is not only sluggish and hesitant but often collusive with those it is supposed to catch. As soon as a scam or scandal surfaces pointing a finger at one politician or another, an army of high profile defenders come up to keep him out of harm's way. If the corrupt happens to be a political big-wig, a web of camouflages, legal, procedural and outright banal, is woven around him as a protective shield which would take a life time for any anti-corruption agency to pierce. Anna Hazare and Arvind Kejriwal are proclaiming loudly from the housetop that if their Jan Lokpal Bill was enacted, 15 Ministers of the central government would be behind the bars. And yet, inspite of a torrent of corruption scandals-Adarsh Housing Society scam. 2G Spectrum, Commonwealth Games, Coalgate not a single big player of the game of corruption was put behind the bars in India (Except, of course, a junior Minister belonging to a coalition partner of the ruling U.P.A. government). That brings out in bold relief the difference between Italy and Japan, on one hand, and India, on the other, in tackling high end corruption.

Coming back to Augusta Westland Choppers scam, another loophole in finalising the deal came to light. It related to flight tests of the choppers. The defence procurement procedure makes it mandatory for trials of the equipments to be purchased to be held in India. It is quite logical because the equipments weapons, transport systems etc. have to operate in different types of terrain and wealther conditions. For instance, no country in the world has an air base at 15,000 feet like India has in Siachen. Similarly, no other country has temperatures varying from minus 10 degrees to 45 degrees celsius.

Accordingly, it was not possible to judge the performance of the Augusta Westland Helicopters at lesser heights. And yet, a rare exception was made in the technical trial of Augusta Westland Helicopter in violation of the established norms of defence procurement procedure. The flight tests termed as Field Evaluation Trials of Augusta Westland helicopters were carried out not in India but in U.K. during January-February 2008. The Evaluation team submitted its report in April 2008 recommending induction of Augusta Westland helicopters into service, on the basis of which the deal was signed in 2010.

That created an impression that, as in the case of purchase of 21 helicopters from the original Westland Company in 1986-88, the very requirement of 12 choppers sought to be purchased from the re-named Augusta Westland Company was a contrived one. The President, Prime Minister and other V.V.I.P's had been carrying on without such helicopters for years and decades. How was it that the need for these arose suddenly in 2007-08 to warrant the purchase order? Was it a case in which the need was created to justify a purchase instead of a purchase proposed to fulfill a need? The chopper deal posed these pertinent questions because unnecessary purchase at the cost of the exchequer benefiting the supplier is also a form of corruption. It would be interesting to find out where the demand originated. Was it the brain child of the Defence Ministry or the Home Ministry, that is, of the Indian Air Force or the National Security Guard? In fact there was a big question mark to the Augusta Westland Copper deal from the very beginning.

Shaken by incessant media exposure of the scam from day to day and offended by opposition's onslaught, the government woke up after sleeping for over a year to take steps for damage control and course correction. There was a flurry of activity in the Defence Ministry and a slew of corrective measures followed. Stung by the slur on his Ministry, the incumbent Defence Minister, known for his personal honesty, went the whole log to adopt corrective measures. Accordingly, Defence Ministry initiated the process of cancellation of the deal. A show cause notice was sent to Augusta Westland on 15 February 2013 seeking cancellation of the contract and taking other actions as per the terms of the contract and the Integrity Pact. Even though three of the twelve helicopters had already been received and around 40-45 per cent of the price paid, further payment was stopped and supply of the remaining choppers put on hold. Further, the Ministry formally asked Finmeccanica, the parent company of Augusta Westland, to state whether any money was illegally paid to any Indian entity or individual which would be violative of the 'Integrity Pact/(That was evidently a formality, as no company would admit that).

Incidentally, the "Integrity Pact" has been reduced to a joke in actual practice. The Integrity clause is provided in every such agreement but the fact remains that it is observed more in its breach than observance.

Another step taken by the Defence Ministry was to make a fresh request to Italy through the External Affairs Ministry for information about the ongoing probe into the scandal. The Ministry also detailed its Joint Secretary-cum-Acquisition Manager (Air) to visit Italy in order to gather as much evidence as possible relating to the charge of payment of bribe by Augusta Westland.

In the midst of all this wild goose chase of the records of Italian probe, the only meaningful action taken in the matter was registration of a Preliminary Enquiry (PE) in the case by the C.B.I. on 25 February 2013 against 13 persons. They included former IAF Chief, S.P. Tyagi and his three cousins Sanjeev, Rajeev and Juli. Others named in the PE were Italian conglomerate Finmeccanicas former CEO Giuseppe Orsi, Augusta Westland CEO Bruno Spagnolini, middlemen Guido Ralph Haske, Christian Michel and Carlo Gerosa. Among their India facilitators in payment of bribe, Aeromatix CEO, Praveen Bakshi and his partner-cum-advocate Gautam Khaitan were also named in the PE. And PE culminated in registration of F.I.R. and regular case against them by the CBI on 13 March 2013.

But that was not going to be the end of the matter. It was going to be a long drawn out process-protracted C.B.I. investigation and court trials. With uncertain results. The opposition political parties as well as a section of the media called it Bofors-II. But what happened in Bofors I? At the end of the day the main culprits and beneficiaries of the scam virtually escaped with zero punishment.

The most sordid part of the Bofor's story was the manner in which the principal accused and beneficiary of the Bofors Gun deal scam, Ottavio Quattrochi, who was a very influential Italian business agent operating in Delhi during mid 1980's, was allowed to go scot free in this case. This has been described candidly by the well known author, Kuldip Nayar in his recently published autobiography entitled *"Beyond the Lines"* Refering to Quattrochi, Kuldip Nayar writes, "He escaped punishment for all he had done and eventually allowed to leave India, the CBI ensuring that no harm came to an individual so close to the dynasty........ According to former CBI Director Joginder Singh, Quattrochi was aware in advance of every move the agency proposed to take against him. For example, he was shown all official papers before he appeared for extradition proceedings at a Malaysian court." About the fact of kickbacks received by Quattrochi in the Bofor's deal, Kuldip Nayar goes on to write, "It was coincidence that one day (3 January 2011) before the CBI was to submit a plea in the court to close the case, the income-tax appellate tribunal pronounced its judgement that Ottavia Quattrochi was the recipient of kickbacks amounting to Rs. 41 crores and demanded that income tax be paid on the income earned".

In spite of the verdict of the income tax tribunal, Quattrochi was let off the hook on the specious plea that it was a civil and not a criminal case. If that was the end result of the much flaunted Bofors Gun deal scandal, only an astrologer can predict the ultimate outcome of the Augusta Westland Chopper scam probe by Indian authorities.

Even as the alleged givers of kickbacks in Augusta Westland Chopper deal were under trial in Italy and the receivers under investigation in India, the important issue thrown up by this case was about the procurement of weapons and equipments in the scam prone defence sector. The question is how to go about it in order to meet the vital requirements of the defence forces. The issue has not been addressed even though it surfaced in a big way in the wake of the Bofors scam. Procurement of arms and equipments cannot be stopped because the country's defence cannot be compromised with. And when a corruption scandal in any such procurement comes to light, it is met with only a negative response from the government-cancellation of the deal and black-listing of the firm in question.

When Augusta Westland scam erupted, the incumbent Defence Minister lamented that, inspite of his punitive measures like blacklisting of several tainted firms, human greed got the better of his sincere efforts and corruption and scams happened. He was right in the sense that in recent years, quite a few firms like Israel Aircraft Industries, Singapore Technoligies and German Rheinmetall have been blacklisted by the Defence Ministry. But that does not address the basic issue of taint free procurement of weapons and equipments needed for the country's defence. How many firms would you blacklist ? If you go on a blacklisting spree, no worth while foreign arms manufacturing firm would be there to buy from. The government seems to be in a bind. How to come out of it?

In one word, the answer is indigenisation in manufacturing of military hardware. It is a sad reflection on India's military-industrial performance that around 70 per cent of our military hardware is procured from foreign arms manufacturers. As a result, India has emerged as the largest market for arms and military equipments in the world making it a happy hunting ground of foreign arms manufacturers. The resultant keen competition among them to beat each other in having a bigger slice of the India defence cake generates corruption all along the line. A recent study by the *Stockholm International Peace Research Institute* has revealed that during the period 2007-11, India accounted for 10 per cent of global arms import, thus making it the largest recipient of foreign arms. In contrast, China which was the largest importer of foreign arms between 2002 and 2006 fell to fourth place in 2007-11. This happened because China had been aggressively forging ahead along the path of indigenisation of its arms acquisitions for quite some time.

A similar course of indigenisation of arms production in India is not only the long-term cure of rampant corruption in defence procurements but also highly beneficial economically. Apart from curbing corruption, indigenisation in military manufacturing would have the additional benefit of generating employment in the country. Large scale purchase of defence equipments from within the country would lead to a massive inflow of money into India's military industrial complex. This would have economically a highly beneficial multiplier effect in employment generation and Research and Development. It is unfortunate that no serious effort has so far been made to develop a robust military industrial complex in the country. The existing institutions of Defence Research and Development Organisation (DRDO), Defence Public Sector Units (DPSUs) and Ordnance Factory Board (OFB) have proved to be restrictive in the path of indigenisation of India's defence production.

These institutions were created at a time when India had no infrastructure whatsoever in the area of defence production. These constituted the foundation store for building up a sound defence production capacity to meet future needs. Instead of serving that purpose, these government controlled institutions have proved to be a stumbling block in creation of a thriving military industrial complex. It is their closed-door exclusivity that has kept the private sector only on the margins of the vast area of defence production. These institutions were created in a zero capacity situation to promote home production of military hardware, but their dog-in-the manger policy has instead retarded the growth of a healthy defence industry in India by keeping the private sector largely out of the gaping field of defence production.

And that at a time when Public-Private Partnership (PPP) model is being increasingly adopted in major infrastructure development projects relating to roads, bridges, power generating units etc. There is no reason why the same should not be done in respect of projects meant for production of weapons and equipments for armed forces. More so when India can boast of having one of the most dynamic manufacturing sectors in the world. The country has any number of entrepreneurs with proven manufacturing capabilities and innovative leadership across diverse industrial segments. Tata Group Companies, Mahendra Group,

Larsen and Toubro, Reliance, to name only a few, are such private sector companies which can meet any challenge thrown up by our defence requirements. For instance, Larsen and Toubro built the hull for India's indigenous nuclear submarine and is in a position to build conventional submarines indigenously.

Inspite of such a vibrant private sector ready to plunge in the ocean of defence production, India continues to be woefully dependent on foreign weapons manufacturers to meet its defence needs. A glaring example of failure of our exclusive and monopolistic Defence Public Sector units to deliver is in the area of production of modern artillery guns. Even though India had technology transfer from Bofors since late 1980's for home production of artillery guns, it has not rolled out an indigenously produced howitzer gun of its own. In fact, eversince Bofors scandal broke up, India has not bought a new artillery gun nor produced one on its own.

Apart from the close-doorish stance of DPSU's, DRDO and ordnance factories, it is rampant corruption in defence sector which is the biggest hurdle in the way of rapid indigenisation of India's arms production. A powerful network of arms dealers and middlemen have developed vested interest in perpetuating India's dependence on foreign arms manufacturers. They have been partnering with foreign firms to sell their wares to Indian armed forces. The middlemen thrive by facilitating the foreign companies to have their way with the corrupt military bureaucratic - political dispensation in India. It is the ugly under-belly of Indian defence procurement which is the real obstacle in the way of indigenisation. The challenge is to have in place a new systemic structure for creating a robust military industrial complex in India.

26

Corruption in India : A Question

In olden times, a king was receiving repeated complaints about a petty official of his darbar indulging in corruption and fleecing his subjects to enrich himself. Being fed up, the king ordered him to sit on the bank of river Ganga and count the waves. The said official, ousted from the king's darbar, established himself on the bank of the river in compliance to the king's order. Sitting on the river bank, whenever he saw a boat sailing along in the river, he stopped it saying that the boat obstructed him in counting the waves of the river for which he was deputed by the king. And he allowed the boat to proceed only after receiving a handsome bribe from the boatman.

The above story illustrates a relevant point. That is, corruption is more a matter of mindset of the corrupt than the opportunities available for it. If the mindset of a people or nation is open to corruption, they would create opportunities for indulging in corruption out of thin air. Like the disgraced official of the king's darbar in the above story. That seems to represent mindset of the people in India today, at least of those who matter and set the standards of social intercourse, in respect of corruption. It poses a pertinent question. Why are we, the people of India, that is Bharat, so prone to corruption as to indulge in it at the drop of a hat or batting of an eyelid?

The question becomes more pointed, as well as painful, in the background of our glorious heritage coming down from an illustrious past. From Adi Shankaracharya to Gautam Buddha to Mahatma Gandhi, India has had a galaxy of bright stars, no other nation in the world could boast of. Adi Shankaracharya rejected the material world as "maya" or illusion to lead mankind to a higher level of blissful existence through the path of renunciation. Buddha again showed the path of right conduct and right goal to attaint 'nirvana' or the state of eternal bliss. And nearer our own times, Mahatma Gandhi's twin mantra of truth and non-violence not only defined his own life but also provided a sound ethical guideline for the people of the country. He talked of *'Satya'* (truth) and '*Ahinsa'* (non-violence) in that order and not 'Ahinsa' and 'Satya'. That is, to the Mahatma, truth came first and non-violence after that.

Gandhi's adherence to truth calls for a little elaboration. He was so much wedded to truth that he called his autobiography *The Story of his "Experiments with Truth"* At the close of his autobiography, the Mahatma observes : "To describe truth as it has appeared to me, and in the exact manner in which I have arrived at it, has been my ceaseless effort......My uniform experience has convinced me that there is no other God than truth......To see the Universal and all-pervading spirit of Truth face to face, one must be able to love the meanest of creation as oneself. And a man who aspires after that cannot afford to keep out of any field of life. That is why my devotion to truth has drawn me into the field of politics...."

That said it all. For the Mahatma, it was his devotion to or pursuit of truth that drew him into politics. How far different is the path of those who enter politics today can better be imagined than described. The fact is that we, the people of India, have undone Gandhi by raising him to the level of sainthood or divinity. We made him a Mahatma, thereby detaching ourselves from him and freeing ourselves from all responsibilities of imbibing even the basics of what he stood for. In no sphere of activity, our distance from him is more noticeable than in the practice of truth as his First Commandment. Ironically, we seem to be as much wedded to untruth or outright falsehood as the Mahatma was wedded to truth.

Shamefully for us our disregard for truth has been highlighted by foreigners who have made forays into India from time to time.

In 1739, the notorious adventurer, Nadir Shah of Persia raided the city of Delhi and caused havoc, killing and plundering the inhabitants for days together. The story goes that when after killing and wounding nearly half of Delhi's population, he paraded the streets of Delhi at the head of a victory procession, the surviving half of the men turned out to greet him with garlands and women showered rose petals from balconies and windows. When Nadir Shah returned to his camp at the end of the victory parade, goes the story, he told his soldiers to run away from the country whose people could be so untruthful. The story may or may not be true, but history records that Nadir Shah did not stay in India and went back to his country with enormous treasure.

In modern times, it was the turn of another foreigner, Lord Curzon, the British colonial ruler, to say it in so many words. Addressing a gathering of academicians and students at Calcutta (now Kolkata) in early 20th century, he was blunt enough to brag that truth was a whiteman's gift to India. It was a piece of his utterly impolitic utterances and manifestation of his paternalistic imperialism which raised a storm. But it did underline the fact that adherence to truth was not one of our strong points. And it could not be brushed aside as Lord Clive's remark earlier that corruption was a way of life in India. Clive said so to defend himself while facing charges of corruption back home in England. Curzon, on the other hand, was making a boastful claim on the basis of what he had observed during his tenure as the Viceroy of India.

It is in this context, that Gandhi's emphasis on truth as the prime value of life has to be viewed. For he saw our weaknesses and shortcomings directly as no other leader did before or after him. As a deeply religious person that he was, Gandhi equated truth with God. Another votary of truth in another land, the English poet Keats, equated truth with beauty when he wrote:

"Truth is beauty, beauty truth
That is all ye know on earth
And all ye need to know."

That was their own way of underpinning the value of truth in social intercourse in accordance with their own predilection.

But truth shorn of divinity and poetic beauty is a simple virtue which one is supposed to live by in normal course in any healthy society. If any society finds it impractible to live with in normal course, there is something grievously wrong with that society. That is the predicament of India which provides for an answer to the pertinent question posed earlier-why are we so prone to corruption? The answer is that once we deviate from the path of truth, there is nothing to stop us from slipping into the mine of corruption. Truth is the *lakshman rekha* which once crossed leaves one free to be corrupt.

For corruption, as we understand it, is end product of a bundle of lies resorted to or indulged in by those involved. Truth, in fact, is the first casualty of a corrupt transaction. In concrete terms, both givers and receivers of illicit gratification or bribes in any transaction have to take course to a series of falsehoods. To hide one wrong act, the corrupt have to invent and resort to a chain of lies. *In that sense, no corrupt person can be truthful and no truthful person can be corrupt.* There is thus an inverse relationship between truth and corruption.

The ease with which our people resort to falsehood in day to day life makes them easily amenable to corruption once they cross the Lakshman Rekha of truth. In ordinary course, there is nothing to stop them from doing so for personal profit at the cost of public good. Here is an example. A well-to-do retired government official was enjoying the benefit of free railway pass entitling him to travel all over the country in air-conditioned comfort for which an ordinary citizen would have to pay through his nose. He had managed to wangle it by resort to a simple falsehood. He had established himself as an old 'freedom fighter' to whom such entitlement was due, without having been anywhere near the freedom movement. And he made no secret of his 'smart act' because it was supposed to be a done thing in his social milieu.

Our politicians spend anything between 20 to 25 lakhs in contesting and winning elections to Parliament and State Assemblies and file return of expenditure of Rs. One lakh or so to keep within the statutory limit. They claim to be residents of places they hardly visit for a few days as outsiders and even manage to procure documentary evidence like ration cards or entry of names in the electoral roll in order to legitimise their election from places they do not belong to but claim to belong. An easy resort to a convenient falsehood which nobody minds does the trick. But once you cross the line and deviate from truth, corruption is within your touching distance.

In such an overwhelming milieu of falsehood, the dictum *'Satyameva Jayate,'* which we have uprooted from our ancient scriptures and planted as our national motto, mocks at us. Evidently, the founding fathers of the Indian Republic were conscious of our scant regard for truth and adopted the above motto as a cautionary insignia. Mahatma Gandhi certainly was. The motto could not be more appropriate, but it is flouted at every step by us. In fact, we seem to delight in indulging in falsehood with 'Satyameva Jayate' being around us as our national symbol. It would be interesting to quote T.N. Seshan, the former Chief Election Commissioner who stole the limelight by his outspokenness during 1990's. In an anguished outburst against corruption in India, he blurted out, "For the benefit of each of you. I request you to rub off that statement below the lions which says *'Satyameva Jayate'* and change it to '*Rishwatameva Jhay-ate'*.

What T.N. Seshan left unsaid was that *'Rishwat* (bribe) was a petrified by-product of deviation from truth. That also explains why we the people of India, in general, and our political power-wielders, in particular, are so prone to corruption. Any amount of outward preventive measures, any number of laws, rules and regulations would fail to curb corruption or our proneness to it. The remedy lies inside us. There is one simple mantra, the Gandhian mantra of truth, which is the real shield to ward off corruption. If only our political power-wielders and government functionaries stick to the principle of truth in all their acts, corruption as we know it can be substantially curbed. Corruption is a malady which has assumed the proportion of an epidemic in India today. Only an effective immune system can prevent its spread. Absolute truthfulness on the part of all stake-holders the people, bureaucrats and the political class is the best immune system against the epidemic of corruption.

27

Judicial Activism Against Corruption and Criminalisation

In recent years, no institution of governance has done so much to check the tide of corruption as India's proactive judiciary. While other anti-corruption agencies like the CBI have faltered, the judiciary has been ever ready to intervene and put them on to the right path in pursuit of cases of corruption on the part of government functionaries. Whenever the investigating agency into cases of corruption is found to be straying under pressure of power that be, the judiciary is there to step in and help in course correction.

The latest example of such corrective intervention by higher judiciary was evident in Supreme Court's close monitoring of investigation of coal block allocations scam. The Supreme Court had directed the CBI investigating into the scam to submit status report of progress in the investigation directly to it without sharing it with the government. When CBI submitted the status report, the central government's counsel initially pleaded that the CBI's status report had not been shared with the Government. The Supreme Court then asked the Director CBI to swear a personal affidavit that the status report was not actually shared with the Central Government. That let the cat out of the bag. The CBI Director being conscious of being hauled up for perjury if he swore a false affidavit admitted that the status report of CBI investigation was not only shared by the government-the Law Minister and officials of the P.M.O. - but was also modified by them. That raised a political storm putting the government on the dock. It resulted in immediate resignation of the government counsel concerned. And after initial resistance, the eventual exit of the Law Minister from the Union Cabinet.

The CBI Director pleaded that as a part of the Central Government, he was duty bound to show the status report to the Law Minister and PMO officials, as asked for, and adopt the changes made by them in the original report prepared by the CBI. The central government saved its face by exiting the Law Minister but it could not escape the ire of the Supreme Court on this unsavory episode. It was in this context that the Supreme Court made the caustic observation that CBI was a "caged parrot" being handled by its masters.

The Supreme Court's "caged parrot" remark not only cast a dark shadow over the functioning of the CBI as a prime investigating agency, but also adversely reflected upon the use or misuse of the CBI by the government in power. The opposition which had always been pointing a finger at the alleged misuse of the CBI by the UPA government, found an unsolicited support in the Supreme Court's pithy observation. It cried foul, as if to say T told you so.' It lent support to all impartial observers who had from time to time pleaded for freeing the CBI from the control of the government in power. As a face saving device, the UPA government started an exercise to ostensibly free the CBI from the control of the government by placing it under an independent Board. Whatever may be the ultimate outcome of the exercise, the Supreme Court has at least induced the government to pay attention to the issue of CBFs independence from the control of the government.

That was an incidental fall out of the highest judiciary's close monitoring of CBFs investigation into the coal block allocations scam. Two back to back judgements delivered by the apex court on two P.I.L's filed by a lawyer, Lily Thomas and N.G.O. Lok Prahari in July 2013 constitute a landmark verdict which would go a long way in preventing the criminalisation and corruption of politics and cleaning up the electoral process. In its first judgement delivered on 10 July 2013, the Supreme Court struck down a provision in the electoral law that protects convicted law maker- M.P's, M.L.C's and M.L.A.'s- from disqualification on the ground of pendency of appeal in higher courts. Section 8 sub-section (3) of the Representation of the People Act debars a person "convicted of any offence and sentenced to imprisonment for not less than two years" from being a legislator. That would cover those convicted and sentenced to imprisonment for two years or more for bribery and corruption as well as other offences like rioting, rape etc. But sub-section (4) of section 8 of the same Act nullifies the disqualification provision by stipulating that if the convicted law maker has filed an appeal against his conviction, he will not be disqualified "until that appeal or application is disposed of by the court." This crippling provision made the disqualification of convicted M.P's/MLA's virtually non-operational. The Supreme Court has just struck down this protective sub-section (4) of section 8 of R.P. Act, holding that the M.P.'s, MLA.'s and MLC's would stand disqualified from the date of conviction itself without waiting for the result of their appeal.

It may be mentioned that the issue of disqualification of law makers convicted of an offence has been discussed at some length in Chapter 15 of this book dealing with Electoral Reforms. And deletion of Sub section (4) of Section 8 of the R.P. Act has been forcefully recommended as a measure of Electoral Reform in order to prevent criminalisation and corruption of politics. It is some consolation that what has been pleaded by this writer in Chapter 15 of this book has now been accepted by the country's higest court of justice. Electoral reforms to curb the criminalisation of politics has long been under discussion at various levels without any concrete step. It speaks volumes about the efficacy of judicial activism that by one stroke of pen the Supreme Court has now ushered in a very important reform to clean up the electoral process.

This monumental Supreme Court verdict is based on sound judicial interpretation of relevant provisions of the constitution. In its 41 page judgement, the court discussed Articles 101 (3) (a) and 190 (3) (a) of the constitution dealing with disqualification of law makers at length and held that Parliament had exceeded its power in enacting section 8 (4) of the Representation of The People. Act. The bench of Juctices A.K. Patnaik and S.J. Mukho padhyaya observed "we also hold the provisions of Articles 101(3)(a) and 190(3)(a) of the constitution prohibit Parliament to defer the date from which the disqualification will come into effect in case of a sitting member of Parliament or a State Legislature. Parliament, therefore, has exceeded its power conferred by the constitution in enacting sub section (4) of section 8 of the (R.P.) Act and accordingly sub-section (4) of section 8 of the Act is ultra vires to the constitution."

As a relief to the sitting law makers who have already filed appeal against their conviction, the verdict would not have retrospective effect. But if any M.P./MLA/MLC is convicted after this verdict, his membership would be suspended with effect from the very date of his conviction.

In the second landmark judgement delivered the next day i.e. 11 July 2013, the apex court ruled that a person who is in jail or police custody cannot contest elections to legislative bodies. The court ruled that only an "elector" can contest the polls and he/she forfeits the right to vote during imprisonment or in police custody. However, the court said that this disqualification would not be applicable to a person subjected to preventive detention under any law. The court based its verdict on provisions of the Representation of the People Act. Sections 4 and 5 of the Act lay down that in order to be elected to Parliament and State Legislatures, the person must be an elector. The court also referred to section 62(5) of the Act which says that no person shall vote at any election if he is confined in a prison, whether under a sentence of imprisonment or otherwise, or is in the lawful custody of police. Reading Sections 4, 5 and 62(5) of the R.P. Act together, the apex court concluded that a person in jail or police custody is not entitled to contest elections.

The Supreme Court passed the order on an appeal filed by the Chief Election Commissioner and others challenging a Patna High Court order barring people in police custody from contesting elections. The apex court observed : "We do not find any infirmity in the findings of the High Court", thus confirming that a person who is not himself an "elector" is not qualified to contest elections to the Parliament or State Legislatures. This verdict would result in a drastic change in the current scenario in which politicians in prison have not only contested but also won elections.

The intelligentsia or politically conscious people in general, for long voicing their grave concern about criminalisation of politics, whole-heartedly welcomed the twin verdict of the apex court. The verdict was sure to strike a popular chord, but the initial reaction of the political class appeared to be confusing. At least some sections of politicians panicked and came out in the open to protest against the verdict. Samjwadi Party general secretary told '*The Times of India*', "We will talk to political leaders for Parliament to amend the constitution so that nobody can stop politicians from contesting elections". (Quoted in '*The Times of India*', Patna edition dated 16 July 2013).

If the politicians did not subvert the twin verdict of the highest judiciary through constitutional amendment or otherwise, it could turn out to be game changer for a cleaner political dispensation. In the ultimate analysis, it is the people of the country who hold the key to crime and corruption free political establishment. For it is the common people equipped with the power of vote who are the final arbiters in a democracy. It is for the voters to exercise their franchise to reject the criminal and corrupt elements at the hustings. If they falter and elect the wrong people being swayed by narrow considerations of caste and creed, they cannot and should not expect a clean political dispensation wedded to common good.

A pithy quotation from the ancient Indian epic 'Mahabharat' would illustrate the point. To the question why the country's immense resources were not benefitting the people, Vidhura told a blind Dhristarashtra, "Having handed over rulership and power to Duryodhana, Shakuni, Kama and Dushyasana, how can you ask for prosperity?" This parable aptly sums up a hard reality of the people electing tainted politicians to rule over them.